'Train your skills, train your body, n[...]
mind. This book will teach you ever[...]
to unlock your full mental potential.'

Ricky Ponting

'This book gives a simple process to be able to use in all
aspects of life and with cricket, to be able to get the best out of
yourself.
I have no doubt in my mind that this book will be able to
help the current crop of cricketers and all future generations
to come.'

Brett Lee

'This mental skills program is so relevant and very specific
with what actually goes on in your mind before you face
every ball. It has really helped me deal with the daily mental
battles that we face in cricket.
It is now a huge part of my daily routine before every
game that I play.'

Faf du Plessis

'The information in this book has helped me out so much.
Not only am I bowling better, I am loving my bowling now,
more than ever.'

Kuldeep Yadav

THE
WINNER'S
MINDSET

THE WINNER'S MINDSET

SHANE WATSON

HarperCollins*Publishers*

HarperCollins*Publishers*
Australia • Brazil • Canada • France • Germany • Holland • India
Italy • Japan • Mexico • New Zealand • Poland • Spain • Sweden
Switzerland • United Kingdom • United States of America

HarperCollins acknowledges the Traditional Custodians
of the lands upon which we live and work, and pays respect
to Elders past and present.

First edition, *Winning the Inner Battle*, published in 2022
by Green Hill Publishing

Second edition published on Gadigal Country in Australia in 2024
by HarperCollins*Publishers* Australia Pty Limited
ABN 36 009 913 517
harpercollins.com.au

A catalogue record for this book is available from the National Library of Australia

ISBN 978 1 4607 6514 2 (paperback)
ISBN 978 1 4607 1704 2 (ebook)

Cover design by HarperCollins Design Studio
Back cover image by Mark Nolan – Cricket Australia/Getty Images
Typeset in Baskerville by Kirby Jones
Printed and bound in Australia by McPherson's Printing Group

To everyone in pursuit of the life they deserve, I hope these pages help you in some way on your journey to finding it.

Contents

Introduction

'I wish I knew then what I know now.' When we get to a certain stage in life we have learnt many hard lessons and gained different perspectives. These thoughts are very common for all of us. Imagine if we only had a little more insight and wisdom at key moments in our life across all aspects of our life. How much more might we have achieved?

On the face of it, I should not really have too many of these types of thoughts. I represented my country more than 300 times. I played cricket successfully all over the world. I was well rewarded for it, had great times, made great friendships, enjoy a comfortable lifestyle now and a great deal of satisfaction from what I achieved. I was at times a controversial cricketer, or at least one about whom people held strong views, which did at times bother me, because

I knew how hard I was trying, how much failure hurt. But that's behind me now.

Or is it? In hindsight, the criticism has a different ring, going beyond whatever the chinks were in my record, like the four Test hundreds, and my various technical and fitness battles. When people got frustrated with me, and I with myself, we were all battling to understand something I only began to understand in the last few years of my career, and have grown to appreciate further while coaching and consulting since: how we can, even with the best intentions, stand in the way of our best performance. One of the oldest sayings in cricket is 'most of the time you get *yourself* out'; a lot of the time in cricket, it is now very obvious to me, we're in a battle with ourselves.

What do I wish I knew then that I know now? I wish I knew how I was mentally sabotaging my own performance.

I wish I knew I was burning mental energy through incorrect focus. I wish I knew how negative mind chatter was controlling me rather than me taking control of that little voice and redirecting the script. I wish I knew about how the human brain can only process one thought at a time – to make sure I was putting the right thought in at the right time so the wrong thought couldn't come in. I wish I had a mental performance model that I could turn to and trust when things went off track.

I never learnt any of these things. Looking back, it is amazing how much emphasis there was on the technical side of cricket and how little on the mental side. I remember doing some mental skills work at 16 years of age in the Queensland under-age Cricket Pathway system. It didn't simplify things enough for me. I had access to sports psychologists in the Australian team. There were pieces of valuable information given there. But I couldn't piece it all together. As a result, I played for 15 years as a professional cricketer repeating the same mental mistakes over and over again.

There were alarm bells early on. I remember at the Australian Under 19 National Championships, playing for Queensland against Victoria, I played an innings where I was paralysed by the fear of failure. I wanted so desperately to score runs and to make the Australian Under 19 team. I became so afraid of getting out that I tied myself in knots trying not to get out. Eventually, after defending everything, I fluffed a cut shot straight to point and was caught.

I missed out on a gift drag down and got out because I was so frozen, so anxious, so focused on the result. I had no understanding of how to bring to this moment all of the technical skills that I had worked so hard on developing. Of how to simply focus on the process and let the results take care of themselves.

I made the same mistakes almost to the very end, including, I remember vividly, in one of my last Test Matches against India in January 2015 at the SCG.

I hadn't scored any runs during that series. I went into that game knowing I was massively under pressure, with the World Cup and an away Ashes series coming up. In the lead-up to that Test match, I got nailed by a journalist at a press conference. The reporter went hard at me, saying, 'Do you think you deserve to be in the team? You haven't scored runs for ages.' Sometimes criticism by the media can be brushed off; this was very hard to do because everyone knew it was true.

I knew going into that Test match that if I didn't score runs my Test career was probably done and potentially then the opportunities in the World Cup at home might have been different.

I fell back into my default mindset for that innings. I reverted to the timid teenager I had been in that Under 19s match, terrified of getting out. I only got as many as 81 in four hours thanks to some generous bowling from Suresh Raina. I got out as indecisively as I batted, holing out to a man I knew was halfway to the fence. It was one of the worst shots I ever played to end one of the worst innings of my career.

It was the final straw. I knew I never wanted to bat like that again. But how could I stop myself? I had no idea, and I played only three more Test matches.

You might be tempted now to think that I'm being too hard on myself and my career. Maybe you'll remember some good things I did. I do too!

The two World Cups, two Allan Border Medals and two Indian Premier League MVPs did not occur by accident – well, not entirely anyway. Sometimes it was the case that circumstances pushed me into the right mindset, and things would 'click' – a very special feeling, of course. But on my own, I now realise, I did not have the mental skills to achieve those states. Peak performance tended to find me, rather than the other way round; I did not understand all of the simple components; I certainly could not repeat them. I looked at other players, really great players, who seemed to do it naturally, but I was never sure what I was meant to be looking at, trying to imitate. My Test career ended with me as much in the dark as ever. Then I had a stroke of luck.

This book has come about because of a chance meeting in 2015 with someone from a very different sport to cricket, Will Power, Australian IndyCar Champion. It is amazing how someone can come into your life out of nowhere and have such an incredible impact on it. Will and I were presenting awards at a Rugby League Awards night and I was sitting next to him.

We started talking about various things, but it very quickly turned to something that Will had been wrestling with for a while – and so had I. Will started talking about how all aspects of his life had been affected by the death of a good friend during a race. It had affected his performances. It had impacted his relationships. It had broken him.

I immediately saw parallels between his experience, and the devastating effect on my generation of cricketers the year before from the death of one of ours.

I had found this extremely difficult to talk about, even to my wife. It had not only intensified the stress of my underperformance on the field but eaten away at my life at home: I was struggling to do things as simple as play in the backyard with our two-year-old son.

It turned out that for the first time in our respective careers, Will and I were trying to overcome a genuine fear for our lives while doing what we loved.

Will, however, had made the decision to do something about it, by consulting Dr Jacques Dallaire, a mental skills guru based in the United States.

Jacques is a well-known performance expert in the motor racing world. He has worked with hundreds of top-level racing car drivers, from F1 to IndyCars. He has also worked with fighter pilots and special forces personnel, as well as high-performing sports people and business leaders, to improve their mental skills in high-pressure environments and achieve their dreams. I wasn't so interested in dreams; I simply wanted a nightmare to end.

Will connected me with Jacques and from our first conversation over the phone I knew I was going to get something very powerful out of working with him. I was so immediately impressed, in fact, that I flew to Charlotte, North Carolina, to enrol in Jacques' mental skills program. I felt it was worth the investment even just for one nugget of gold that could help me in my next life as a cricket coach, which at that time was what I really wanted to do once my playing days had finished.

Two days. That was all it took: two days. It's two days I now wish I had had at the start of my career rather than towards the end, but it was two days I will never forget.

I had spent 20 years around sports psychologists and mental skills coaches, but either I had not been in the right frame of mind or what they told me had not resonated. What Jacques said was so practical and so memorable, I felt like I had seen past the 'what' and the 'how' to the 'why' of sport.

For the next four years, as I finished off my white ball career with Australia and played in the best T20 leagues around the world, I became obsessed with Jacques' teachings, applying them to complex game situations and high-level pressure. The result was that I played the most consistently successful and enjoyable cricket of my life in my mid to late 30s, and when I eventually got into coaching I found this the most stimulating part of the job – coaching the individual, not just the player.

Working recently as an assistant to Ricky Ponting at the Delhi Capitals, I have been fascinated by the difference between the importance of mental skills and the way they are coached. The thing about the IPL is that the players are already really good. Their skills are incredible. Their fitness, their power, their dedication are just about as good as they can be. So why coach them as though they're bits of machinery? I strongly believe that the next step in cricket's evolution will not be in coming up with new ramp shots or mystery balls, or crunching more data or making better plans. It will be training cricketers' minds, so that they can reproduce their skills under pressure or execute team strategies more consistently.

The mental skills that you will learn in this book aren't just about cricket either – they are totally universal and can be applied to any aspect of your life. Whether it is bringing your best performance to your study, your work, your sporting endeavours, your relationships or your parenting, this information will help unlock all of the skills that you have inside you, to bring the best version of yourself to every performance that you have, especially when the chips are down and your performance really matters.

One of the things we most love about sport is how it gives expression and provides an outcome for the day-to-day business of being better. When I say I wish I had known then what I know now, I mean it in all aspects of my life, and I hope you'll find this information as stimulating and even revolutionary as I have.

1

Skillset Versus Mindset

Why do we perform poorly even when we are incredibly well prepared?

There is a really simple question we often ask ourselves. Why do we perform poorly even when we are incredibly well prepared? Cricketers will often say, 'I was so well prepared, I trained so well, did all the right things the night before, so why did it not translate into runs or wickets?'

Cricket is full of these types of stories: here is one of mine. There was a legspinner I used to play grade cricket with. He played indoor cricket for Australia. He would bowl in the nets at training and it was like he was Shane Warne. He landed everything − leggies, wrong uns, sliders − they all landed perfectly. This guy was an absolute genius in the nets. But then he would get to the game and he would struggle. He would bowl a few full tosses, a double bouncer here and there but would land some good deliveries every now and then. He would then go back to the nets the following week and be able to land them perfectly again almost without fail. He would rip them past me like Shane Warne did. I always thought to myself, I wonder what's going on with him? How can he be so good in the nets but struggle so much in the games? Obviously, the problem lay in his mind as he definitely had the skills. But what exactly was happening in his mind? And why was it happening?

This is why it is so important to understand the concept of skillset versus mindset, and how the two are correlated. There are two aspects to this which are really important to understand.

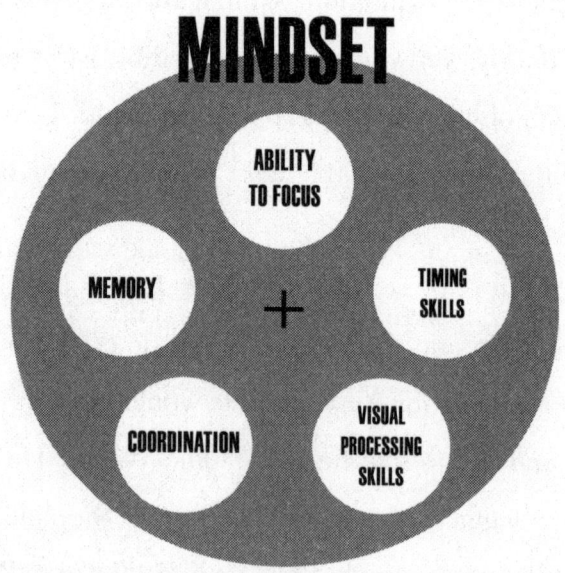

Skillset is everything that you learn and develop. It's your hand–eye coordination, memory, timing skills, your visual processing skills, and your ability to focus. These are the core elements that go into learning your skill. Learning the technical skills is a vital part of being a successful cricketer, as it is for anything that you want to be good at. It is vital in any pursuit of knowledge or information that you are trying to embed in your mind. It is all the information that you have inside your mind, the technical skills that you have developed, the skills that you work so hard to acquire. Repetition of these technical skills over long periods of time builds up your muscle memory.

But skillset is separate from mindset. Mindset is the mental environment in which our skills are expressed. It's important to understand that if your mindset is incorrect or corrupted, then the ability to access all the skills you have developed is significantly reduced to a point where you cannot access those skills at crucial moments in time.

Let me explain an incorrect or corrupted mindset by recalling one of mine. In 2015, my mindset shifted significantly and it was nowhere near where it should have been while I was facing fast bowling. When I was at my best, my mental environment was very positive and aggressive to react as quickly as I could to the ball coming down. I had no premeditation at all and I just trusted my instincts completely that I would play the necessary shot to that ball. Whereas, at this point in time, I was fearful of the ball coming down. I was premeditating the ball was going to be short, which, for every batter, is the opposite of the mental environment that you want to have to access all of your technical skills. This coincided with a time where my performances tanked in a big way due to my incorrect mindset. I had the skillset deep inside of me from all of the hours that I had spent refining my technique since I was a kid, but my mindset was totally corrupted, which meant I couldn't access a lot of those ingrained skills.

As soon as I created the right mental environment again, I went back to playing fast bowling, and the short ball in particular, as well as I ever had before. I will explain how I did it in more detail as we go.

It's very important to understand how tightly correlated skillset and mindset are. This whole book is based on how to instil the correct mindset and how to create the right mental environment, so that – whenever you want – you can access all of the skills you have developed.

This incorrect mindset occurred throughout my career prior to meeting Jacques, especially when things didn't go to plan and my performances started to wane. I would start thinking: 'Yeah, I've lost it. I haven't played my pull shot for a few games, I just keep mis-hitting balls that normally I would nail – where has it gone?!'

But after learning this information, I completely understood how to create the correct mental environment and how to redirect it so, all of a sudden, the skills that I had worked so hard on were instantly accessible again.

It is also important to deeply understand that your best technical self, your skillset, as well as your best mental self, your mindset, are connected. If your mental environment is spot on but the technical side of your game is slightly off, then your ability to access all of your skills is reduced. Likewise, if your technique is absolutely spot on but your mental environment is not right, then your ability to access your technical skills is also significantly reduced.

For example, the innings that I played in the 2015 World Cup Quarter Final against Pakistan stands out as one where I had a technical deficiency that was getting me into trouble even though my mental environment was spot on. I was locked in the battle with my mate Wahab Riaz. Technically, I was too closed off to the ball. Wahab, a left-armer, was jamming me up. Every short ball he bowled, which was four out of every over, was fast, and he was so accurate with his length and line. It was like I had a black spot to the short ball climbing into my left armpit. Steve Smith was facing him as well and had no problems. But because of my technical deficiency in that game, no matter how good my mindset was, I was getting into trouble and in the end I got very lucky. I could have been out a number of times, with one big moment being a mis-timed hook shot that flew straight to fine leg. Fortunately it was dropped and I was able to go on to score a few more runs.

I believe every time you go out to play, every ball you face or bowl, you need to be aware of your crucial technical cues. I will outline what my technical cues were later on. You have to be as technically correct as possible to execute your skills to the best of your ability, and you need to combine this with creating the correct mental environment for you. This is what I was chasing every ball. I was always aware of my technical cues, as I grew up being a technically driven cricketer and this is what coaches had helped me with. But once I understood the best mindset for me that I needed to create every ball, then I was just trying to pull the two components together, and when I did, the best version of me was always on display.

It's important, as a starting point, to understand that skillset and mindset work together.

KEY TAKEAWAYS

- Skillset is all the skills we develop through hard work and repetition.

- Mindset is the mental environment around all of this skillset.

- If our mindset is flawed, our ability to access these skills is significantly reduced.

2

The Human Mind –
The Iceberg

What are the powerful functions of the human mind that I can access all of the time?

I am going to distil the complexity of human psychology into simple terms so that you can understand and see the power of it, to then apply it to your own performance.

There are two key dimensions of the human mind, and these are the very simple but incredibly important components of the human brain and their function – and you won't need to have a psychology degree to understand them.

The iceberg analogy is often used in psychology to explain how the two key components of the human mind work together.

Imagine you are on a boat drifting towards an iceberg. What you can see of the iceberg above the surface of the water, what's conscious to you, is the conscious mind.

The unconscious mind is what is under the water, what you can't see. It's this huge mass of ice, so much bigger than what you can see above the surface. You can also think of the surface of the water as the boundary of our conscious awareness.

The reason why the iceberg is such a powerful analogy for the human mind is because, as powerful as our conscious mind is, our unconscious mind is many, many times more powerful.

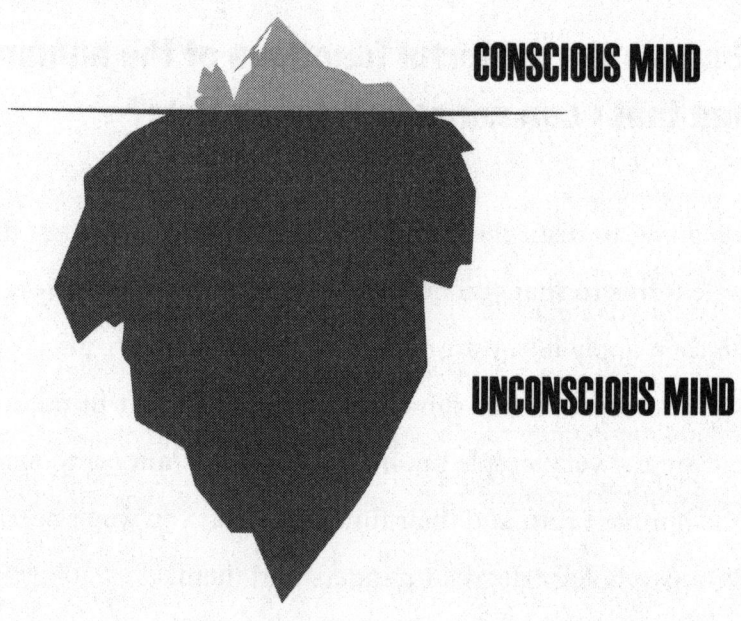

CONSCIOUS MIND

UNCONSCIOUS MIND

The conscious mind – the skipper

The conscious mind is the captain of the ship. It directs where you go. It acts like the rudder on a boat, or the steering wheel on a car, or even a cricket captain setting the field.

It directs your mind to where it goes. And it's in control because it's the captain of the ship.

Its wheelhouse is analysing, deciding, problem-solving or calculating various things. Problem-solving is one of the conscious mind's major strengths. You can be very much inside your mind when using your conscious mind.

The most important and the most powerful part of the conscious mind is understanding that *we are in control of it.*

Most of us don't exercise the control we have, and also fail to make the most of the control we have. Most of us allow our environment around us to dictate how we think and where our mind goes. That's why most people tend to be 'good' when things are going well but fall to pieces and sabotage themselves when they're not.

But the fundamental truth is: we are actually in control of our conscious mind, if we want to be.

The mind chatter, that little birdie on your shoulder that is always talking to you, that internal dialogue you have with yourself, that is a conscious mind function, which means that *you are in control* of what that little birdie is saying.

We are in control of that mind chatter. And that's an incredibly powerful thing to understand. If we want to take control, if we want to exercise control over our thoughts, we can simply redirect the script of the little birdie.

But again, most of us just allow the environment around us to dictate how we think. We need to listen in to what's going on inside our own head, to what that internal monologue is, and then try to shift it to the right thought at the right time.

Cricket has lots of little sayings that are drummed into us from an early age, and they influence our thinking. A great example is: 'Now's not a good time to get out. We just lost a wicket. Make sure we don't lose back-to-back wickets.'

We immediately start directing our mind towards the fear of getting out, instead of thinking: 'Let me just react to the ball coming down. If it's a loose ball in my zone, I'm going to be all over it. If it's not, I will instinctively defend it.'

You could have been a part of a 200-run partnership and your mate just got out. As soon as the team loses a wicket, your mindset changes to: 'We can't lose two wickets back-to-back.' Even though you're in a space where you're batting really well, your mindset shifts straight away.

That's the mind chatter. We need to understand how to redirect it, so you're moving your thoughts in the right direction towards what you need at that moment in time to have full access to your skills.

Prior to understanding this information, I was terrible at controlling my conscious mind and especially that little birdie sitting on my shoulder chatting to me.

We all have a battle that we need to try to win every day and every performance. That battle is with that little birdie on our shoulder. Some days, that birdie is whispering and is very easy to redirect, whereas other days, that voice can feel like it is so loud that it is shouting at you and is incredibly hard to redirect to the right thought to create the best possible mental environment. I had days where that battle was nearly impossible to win and I lost, which had a massive impact on me bringing the best version of myself to every ball. But other days, I made the most of the control that I had and ball after ball I kept redirecting my mind to the right thoughts. The more we work on winning this battle, the softer and softer this voice will become and this is when mastery of your mind is front and centre. This is what we are all chasing. To win this battle more consistently, we need as much mental energy as possible, to grab control of that little birdie and redirect your thoughts to the right thing at the right time to perform at your best. I will talk much more about this later on.

A good example of where I lost the battle was an IPL game in 2013. I was playing for Rajasthan Royals against Sunrisers Hyderabad. We were chasing only 137. I fell into the trap of changing my mindset every time we lost a wicket.

My mindset immediately turned defensive because I was always taught that we needed to consolidate every time we lost a wicket, to build another partnership. We lost a wicket in the 9th over while I was out there and I went into my shell. Just as I was about to take the game on again, we lost another in the 12th over and I went back into my shell again. By the time I holed out in the 14th over for 11 in 20 balls, having faced 10 dot balls, the run-rate had climbed out of control and the game was lost. That game stands out, as I missed so many opportunities to score because I was thinking about how we needed to build another partnership and to give myself five or six balls each time to build a new partnership. I let the environment dictate how I played. I didn't control my conscious mind to redirect the script into the right mindset for me to be at my best, which was having an aggressive mindset and putting pressure on the bowler for them to know if they bowled something loose I was going to be all over it.

A common pitfall for T20 batters today is the mindset of being content to get off strike. You see that their body language, their bat swing, their energy and intent is geared to being content with one; at best, they might pick up two. All the while they are missing out on loose balls from the bowler that they could put away for a boundary. But when we are looking to score, putting pressure on the bowler to score, we have the intent, the body language, the bat swing to be all over a loose ball to put it away, hit it for a boundary, a four or six, or three or two and then if it isn't a loose ball, we then can instinctively defend it for a single or maybe even a dot ball.

There is such a significant difference in mindset from defensive to offensive and by understanding which is the correct mindset for you, to redirect your mind to the best version of you, then you have access to all of the shots that you have worked so hard to develop and will not be restricting yourself by only looking for singles.

The unconscious mind – the loyal crew

The function of the unconscious mind is that it acts as the crew. Whatever the captain (the conscious mind) says, the crew simply responds, 'Yes skip, I've got it, I'll take you there.'

Unlike the fielder who occasionally drifts out of position after the captain places him there, the unconscious mind follows the captain's orders no matter what. It's not there to debate whether the captain is right or wrong.

If your mind chatter says, 'You've lost it' or 'You always fail against this team or at this ground', your unconscious mind is not there to rebut and say, 'No, last time you played well and you've got the skill to overcome that record.'

What I learnt is that we can't directly control our unconscious mind.

We can definitely influence it. But we can't directly control it.

Despite simply following orders, the unconscious mind is vital. The crazy power of the unconscious mind is that it keeps us alive. It keeps our heart beating. It performs cellular repair. It does a great deal while we're asleep, while we're unconscious.

When you break it down to those simple definitions, you realise this is a huge, incredibly powerful tool that we need to tap into.

That's why the iceberg, the mass under the water, the unconscious mind, is such a great analogy.

The most important thing with the unconscious mind from a performance standpoint is that this is where our best performances live.

When we're at our absolute best, when we get in the flow, or we get 'in the zone', our unconscious mind takes over and integrates all of the motor and sensory inputs to create these moments of performance virtuosity. We get out of our own way and direct ourselves into the right mental space where we can tap into all the skills we've got inside us, and then just let it flow. That's the power of the unconscious mind. Our best performances sit below the surface and not in the conscious mind above the water.

So how can we direct our thoughts to influence the unconscious mind, to then access all of our skills to achieve our best performances?

Once you understand that you are in control of your conscious thoughts, then you have to work on the skill of redirecting the script. Whenever the little birdie pops up with negative thoughts or the wrong thoughts, listen in for those thoughts, identify them and redirect them straight away.

There was an innings that really stands out to me where I harnessed all of this awesome information and tapped into the power of the unconscious mind. This was the first time that I ever pulled myself into 'the zone' instead of hoping that all the planets aligned and I fell into the zone, which fortunately had happened quite a few times throughout my career up until this point.

It was the 2018 IPL Final when I was playing for the Chennai Super Kings against the Sunrisers Hyderabad. We batted second and we were chasing 179 and, before I knew it, I had soaked up 10 balls without scoring. But during these first

10 balls, I was working through my technical cues, to make sure they were all locking in every ball and, as importantly, my mental cues to create the correct mental environment to tap into the power of my unconscious mind. I was critiquing every ball. How was my intent? Was I really aggressive? Am I just reacting to the ball coming down at me? Ball by ball I was pulling myself into the zone. But I was super aware of what the birdie on my shoulder was saying.

It had turned negative when my opening partner, Faf du Plessis, had got out taking on a risky shot, as he felt we needed to get on with it because of my shockingly slow start. I had caused Faf to take a risk he didn't have to take. I was super aware of what the birdie was saying: 'You caused that, now is the time to get on with it or get out.' I just had to keep ignoring it, in order to focus on my execution in the moment, to bring the best version of me every single ball and let the results look after themselves. And before I knew it, I got away by continuing to pull myself into the right mindset and exercise the control that I had over my conscious mind. And once I got there I stayed there, by ensuring that I kept the exact same mindset of being aggressive, with no premeditation, and trusting my instincts. Before I knew it, the game was done and I had scored 117 not out from 57 balls and CSK had chased down 179 with nine balls to spare.

I will explore this innings in further detail later in the book, because I used all of the mental skills that I outline in this book to bring together the best version of myself under extreme pressure.

Unconscious mind exercise – controlling our emotions

To prove how the unconscious mind is more powerful than our conscious mind, I would like you to do an exercise.

The unconscious mind serves as the reservoir of our emotions. Our emotions are not a conscious mind function. We 'feel' as a result of our unconscious mind acting on the thoughts that we set in our conscious mind.

How do you feel happy, and not just look happy?

The only way you can accomplish this is to first think of 'happy' thoughts in your conscious mind.

You need to place a happy thought, a picture of a happy place, or think of a happy memory in your mind and play that thought, picture, or memory out. Try it and see what happens. Your emotions react to this happy thought and you feel happy.

This is the conscious mind, the captain of the ship, thinking about a happy moment in your life, and then the unconscious mind, the crew, says 'I can take you there' and you start to feel happy.

This is how some actors and actresses genuinely make themselves cry in a scene. They think of a very sad moment in their conscious mind and the feeling part in the unconscious mind is so strong that they genuinely do cry sad tears.

That's a really simple way to influence your unconscious mind. And as simple as that example is, that's actually how you tap into your unconscious mind during the best performances. This is at the core of the ACT Model process that is an unbelievably powerful process that changed my life completely. I see the ACT Model as the magic dust to bring the best version of yourself to every situation. I will explain the ACT Model process in further detail later on in the book. But simply put, it is a conscious mind rudder control process that puts you in control of your thinking to bring out your best performances when you need them most.

The conscious and unconscious mind are the two fundamental aspects of the human mind. Honestly, those two components alone, in a really simple format, are all you need to know to be able to understand how to make your mind work for you and move it in the right direction. It also allows you to understand what you can control, what you can't control, and how to influence your mind to get the best results that you possibly can and bring the best version of you. It is the perfect foundation for what we will learn next.

KEY TAKEAWAYS

- The conscious mind is the captain of the ship.

- We are in control of our conscious mind.

- Mind chatter, the little birdie on our shoulder, is a conscious mind function, so we are in control of what that little birdie is saying.

- The unconscious mind is the crew of the ship.

- We can't directly control the unconscious mind, but we can influence it.

- The unconscious mind is where all of our best performances sit.

3

Trusting Your 'Gut Feel'

What the hell is 'gut feel' and how do I access it?

How many times have you been told throughout your life, 'just trust your gut'? I would ask myself, what the hell does that mean? But having finally been educated on the conscious and unconscious mind functions, I now know exactly what they mean and the power of the 'gut feel'.

We've established that the conscious mind is a problem solver. It's amazing at processing data. In cricketing terms, it is like poring over statistics and video footage to analyse where the best spot is to bowl to a certain batsman.

We know the unconscious mind has a deep, deep reservoir of knowledge and feelings. We can't access it directly but we know it's there. Everything we experience in our lives, everything we see, is taken in by our conscious mind and stored deep in our internal computer, our unconscious mind.

We're not even aware that it's happening, but it's processing information. And then all of a sudden, our gut tells us something. We have some intuition, or we gain insight. We're not sure why we came to that conclusion, but it feels right, and 99 per cent of the time it is right. Both the conscious and unconscious mind are processing information, but one is on a more conscious deliberate level where we direct our thoughts to something like a data spreadsheet. In other instances, it's just a case of observing an environment or a situation and starting to get a feel for it, using our intuition to make assessments.

The latter is trusting your gut.

Malcolm Gladwell wrote a book about what we sometimes call intuition, or instinct, called *Blink: The Power of Thinking without Thinking*. I had read it well before I learned about the power of the unconscious mind and I found it fascinating. Although I didn't fully understand why this was the case, what it actually meant and how I could tap into it myself. But this powerful information reinforced what I read and I then knew what trusting your gut truly meant and how to implement it.

My simplest example of testing the 'gut feel' in cricket came over the last two years of my bowling career in T20 leagues around the world. I used it while deciding what was the right ball to bowl at the right moment in time to each specific batter.

If I used my conscious mind to decide what the right ball was at the right moment in time, I would be standing at the top of my mark recalling the previous balls that I had bowled to that player, or that type of batter, throughout my career and the results of those various balls to then choose the right ball at that moment. To decide on the right ball to bowl at that exact moment in time could take hours.

Whereas if I just put my mind on neutral (something I will explain how to do later on), allowed space to feel what the right ball was for that moment, and trusted what I felt was the right ball to bowl and committed to that fully, then 99 per cent of the time it was the perfect ball to bowl at that moment. I was tapping into the power of the unconscious mind, which had automatically processed every ball that I had bowled to that type of batter and the correct answer popped up without too much mental energy being exerted.

Even though I couldn't articulate why it was the right ball, my unconscious mind was giving me the answer as I was allowing space for it to appear.

I went from bowling pretty well in games over the previous couple of years to, all of a sudden, having my most successful year with the ball culminating in my best ever IPL returns in

2016. I took 20 wickets and finished third on the leading wicket-takers for that season at the ripe old age of 34. My skill was the same as it always had been, but my decision-making was the best it had ever been, as I was tapping into the unconscious mind's decision-making power. And then, step two was fully committing to that ball by being singularly focused on the technical aspect to execute that ball to the best of my ability, and just repeating this every ball each game. I didn't become more skilled out of nowhere. I was just using these new mental skills I had learnt, and wow, what a difference they made!

This example is how I started to access the power of the unconscious mind from a bowling perspective, but here is how I really started to tap into the power of the decision-making process from a batting perspective. There was a quality allrounder from Sri Lanka, Thisara Perera, who I used to enjoy facing. I felt a lot of the time that I matched up very well to him and could take him down because he bowled at a nice hitting pace, with a flatter trajectory, and he didn't always execute once I got on top of him. Normally, I would face one ball and say to myself, 'OK, he is bowling like he normally does, so I feel that I can line him up today.' I would then go after him, normally with great results. But then on other days, I would face one or two balls and it would just feel a little different. Whether it was his pace was better on that day, the ball was reacting differently off the wicket, or the viewing conditions were just a little different on that day, something didn't feel right. If I let my emotions take over and say to myself, 'I normally take him down, so no matter what, let's take him down again today', it always ended badly. Whereas when I trusted my gut feel, whether it felt right that I could line this guy up or whether just on that day, something was slightly different, the outcome was normally so much better.

With some other bowlers that I had faced in the past, who I struggled against and felt like I couldn't line up, whether it was because of their pace, their angle, their ability to expose my weaknesses, there were days where it just felt different. I would face a couple of balls and feel, 'Oh today I can definitely line this guy up.' But if I didn't trust my gut and question it with, 'No, this guy is not the guy I can take down as he normally gets me out and is able to expose my weaknesses', then I wasn't making the most of the situation and capitalising on this opportunity to score more freely off him.

Now that I have moved into the coaching side of the game, this is one of the most important things that I instil in the players that I'm working with. Always trust your gut feel. Don't let anyone get in your way to cloud your judgement of your gut feel decision-making power. You know better than anyone on the planet what the right ball is to bowl at that moment in time, or the right bowler to take down at that moment in time. If you are allowing space in your mind for your gut feel to make the right decision at the right time, then good outcomes will usually follow. Sometimes captains can try to override your gut feel by directing you to bowl a ball that is different to what you are feeling. But only you know what the right ball is at that moment in time, because you are the one who has been bowling so many balls to so many different batters since you were a kid. Only you know, deeply through your experiences, some of which produced potentially painful consequences, what the right ball is for that moment.

So the captains out there need to be very aware of when the right time is to direct a bowler or when to leave them alone to allow the power of the gut feel to do its thing.

The last common example regarding gut feel from a batting perspective came up a couple of times in my first season of coaching with the Delhi Capitals. It brought back memories of the exact situation that I experienced during my first season playing at Royal Challengers Bangalore in 2016.

I was in the middle batting with one of my favourite cricketers of all time, the great AB de Villiers. We were chasing and I was a little sluggish at the start of my innings. Then the perfect match-up came my way. The bowler was someone who I knew I could definitely take down and I had to capitalise on this opportunity in the game. But then AB said something to me. AB is the sweetest guy I have ever played cricket with and his words were coming from the right place. He said, 'Let's just take this game a little deeper. You don't need to take this guy on right now.' All of a sudden, I started to question my gut feel. Was it the right time? Is this guy really the right match-up? Maybe I shouldn't take this guy down? Before I knew it, I had half-committed to a shot and hit one straight up and got out. I remember walking off thinking, 'Why didn't I just trust what I felt?', instead of letting an outside influence get in the way of the superpower of trusting my gut feel in making decisions for me. As the bowler was coming in, I was fighting myself via that little voice, 'You should go! No you shouldn't! AB said to take it a little deeper!' When this confusion is going on in your mind, bad things normally happen.

So, individually, we need to deeply trust our gut feel and not allow any influences around you to direct you away from the power of this decision-making process. It can be very difficult at times, as I found out in that game for RCB. Trust what we feel and then commit to it with 100 per cent conviction. From a bowling perspective, it is important to chat to your captain and make sure that they trust you to commit 100 per cent to your gut feel unless you need some guidance, in which case you need to reach out for their help. On the other hand, we need to be very careful to not get in the way of a teammate who is tapping into this superpower as well, by influencing or planting a seed of doubt that could have an impact on their ability to execute their skill at that moment in time.

KEY TAKEAWAYS

- Gut feel is the superpower of decision-making.
- Once we feel the right decision, we need to commit 100 per cent to what we feel.
- Don't let any outside influences get in the way of your gut feel decision-making process.

4

Confidence, Focus and Overcoming Fear

What are the things that prevent you from bringing the best version of yourself to any performance?

There are two very important questions that we need to answer. What gets in the way of your best performance? And, what are the things that prevent you from bringing the best version of yourself to any performance?

Even high-performing individuals ask these questions. The answers typically revolve around self-doubt, fear of failure, and lack of confidence. Distractions or a lack of focus can come into it as well.

Following on from those answers, more questions usually arise. How do I remain confident when things aren't going well? How can I focus more effectively? And if I lose focus, how do I regain it?

Confidence and fear of failure were two major reasons why my career ebbed and flowed so much in terms of performance. Like a lot of people, I was only as good as my last few results.

If I was doing really well, if I was scoring runs and taking wickets, my confidence was sky high. I was riding a wave, the outcomes were great, and I felt bulletproof. That even flowed into other parts of my life, which is known as circumstantial confidence.

When my confidence was high, I could miss out in a few games with the bat and I would not worry or even think about it. I just went into the next game taking the game on with no fear.

Whereas the other side of the equation, if things aren't going well and results have been bad for a while, then other things in your life can start to really affect you even further. You take issues more to heart. You start doubting yourself in all aspects of life.

In cricketing terms, when my confidence was low I started to worry about failing. I would start to worry that I might get dropped and then start to think about what would happen if I was dropped.

How many cricketers define themselves and their daily confidence levels by their scores or their figures? That's what happens when our confidence is based on results. And we all know that when our confidence is high, we normally have our best performances.

This can also feed into our focus. When we're confident, our focus is sharp and unwavering. When we're not confident, our attention can get distracted pretty easily. The mind chatter starts to occur. We start listening to the negative thoughts as they get louder and louder and the fear of failure creeps in. These are the most common issues that everyone wrestles with.

When we start to doubt ourselves or fear that we might fail, our focus of attention shifts from what we are doing to the consequences of what we are doing and our performance usually suffers.

For us to be at our best, we know our confidence needs to be high. But if we're basing it around results only, are we building our confidence around the right thing? Because, if we know anything about cricket, it's that outcomes go up and down, and the margins between success and failure are fine.

Some of the best players to have ever played the game, like Shane Warne and Ricky Ponting, had a ratio of good to bad games of around 40–50 per cent good versus 50–60 per cent bad. Shane took three wickets or more in a Test innings 52 per cent of the time and he was arguably the greatest ever. Ricky made 50 or more with the bat only 36 per cent of the time and he is the second-highest Test run-scorer ever. So where does that leave us mere mortals? Somewhere around 20–30 per cent for good games and 70–80 per cent for bad is an excellent result. We can't ride the waves of confidence off 20–30 per cent good results and 70–80 per cent bad results that are always going to happen. Because if we do, our confidence is only going to be high 20–30 per cent of the time, which is not good at all. Instead, we have to base our confidence around the right things so that we can be at our best as consistently as possible.

Because confidence is such a key issue, we need to understand the two critical things that contribute to it.

The first is your preparation. It's knowing that you've ticked every box in the lead-up to a game.

England's Kevin Pietersen was one of the most confident players I ever played against. He explained to me on my podcast *Lessons Learnt with the Greats* that his incredible confidence came from his preparation:

I was at my best when my practice was flawless. And that's basically it. I never substituted anything for hard work. I never went to bed the night before a Test match or a One Day International thinking, 'Oh my goodness, why didn't

I practise my sweeps today if I'm going to sweep him tomorrow. I'm playing Harbhajan Singh tomorrow.' Or, 'How's my pull shot looking? I've got Brett Lee tomorrow at the Gabba and I cannot play the pull shot.'

That is what confidence from preparation looks like. Conversely, we've all experienced the flip side of that, where we haven't hit the ball that well, or the ball isn't coming out that well at training. We know things aren't right. We carry that doubt or lack of confidence into the game.

Deep down we know how we trained on a particular day and whether we are deeply confident about where our skills are at. But just because we didn't train perfectly the day before the game doesn't mean we can't walk out to the middle and be at our best. There are so many factors that can change from the preparation day to the game day, one of which is just being human. You can just be slightly off for no apparent reason. It's just a not-so-good day.

Sometimes you can have a coach standing next to you in the nets yelling 'great shot' when they think you have middled the ball, or 'well bowled' when they think you have executed that ball perfectly. The coach always means well, as they are trying to help build your confidence, but only you know deep down whether you are right on with your skill execution or not.

The second key element relating to confidence, the one that catches most people out, is our focus. What are we focusing on at the moment of our performance? Have we taken that confidence into the moment of performance or are we starting to doubt ourselves in some way when it is go time?

While feeling well prepared certainly contributes to our levels of confidence that we might take into a match, it doesn't guarantee that we'll be confident during that match. If prior preparation guaranteed that we would have high levels of confidence at match time, we'd never see situations where players who are well prepared sometimes still 'choke' when the pressure to perform is on. Confidence is built with our preparation, but we then need to hold onto that high level of confidence when everything is on the line during the game.

KEY TAKEAWAYS

- Confidence is integral to everyone's best performances.
- We build our confidence through our preparation.
- We need to maintain this high level of confidence when it is game time.
- We normally build our confidence levels around results, but these do ebb and flow significantly.
- So are we building our confidence around the right thing?

5

The Performance Equation: A × B = Results

How do we get the best results that we possibly can every time we need to perform?

No one wants to be a loser. No one wants to fail.

I've never known anyone to say, 'I just want to suck. I want to be junk at something' or 'I want to have a really bad day today!'

Everyone wants to be successful. Everyone wants to be at the top. Everyone wants to get the best results they possibly can and have all of the trimmings that come with being the best.

But the one thing I have come to know is that being totally focused on the outcome was the biggest obstacle to me achieving what I wanted.

Of course, this goes against what we're brought up to believe. Society teaches us that it's good to worry about results, that we should worry about results, that we should not only feel it but we should also act out those feelings if we fail. Because it proves that we care, right? Because if you don't see somebody who gets bent out of shape when they don't get the result they're striving for, the first thing we think about is they're not hungry enough. They don't want it badly enough. They don't really care. In cricket, this is commonly expressed in the culture of blowing up with anger when you have been dismissed, or after you have bowled a bad spell. If you don't blow up and tear the dressing room up it means that you supposedly don't care. And the other side of it is if someone comes in from being dismissed and does lose their mind and lets loose with rage it supposedly shows they really care.

I definitely developed the habit of getting angry after I got out. It just became so ingrained in me. I hated losing. I hated being dismissed and I would show it to everyone including myself that I cared. This was my learned behaviour.

It was common, but it wasn't the only approach. Damien Martyn, an incredible batter that I played with and one of the most graceful players that I have seen, never used to throw the toys out of the cot when he got out. He would just come in, sit down, and be a little frustrated. But he wouldn't say anything. He wouldn't throw anything and then he just got on with it. He wouldn't be happy and smiley but he certainly wouldn't lose his mind with rage either.

Because of how I was programmed, it was easy to think he didn't really care. I came to realise that he cared as much as everyone else, but he didn't necessarily show it by losing it in the change room after he got out. He never put it into words, but Damien seemed to understand that this kind of performative rage was not only pointless, but actually counterproductive – it certainly didn't help you do better next time.

Ok, so how do we create the best results possible? The answer is this performance equation: A × B = Results.

Understanding the fundamental truth of this performance equation was a lightbulb moment for me. Before I go any further I should stress, over the next few paragraphs it might seem like results don't matter at all. That's definitely not the case. Results are very important. We all want to be successful and I personally want to be as successful as anyone else on the planet. This book is all about how to get the best results possible. So I really do care about results, as we all do.

But the key piece to understand is that if you focus exclusively on the outcomes and tie your emotions to that, then it will be much more difficult to get the results you want. The key to getting the best outcome is having the 'correct focus'. The correct focus isn't on the results, it's on the things you can control, and the thing that you control fully is the execution of the process associated with your performance – in the moment when it's required.

Once I understood this performance equation, and it took me a few hours to deeply understand, it had a profound impact on me. Because it lifted a huge weight off my shoulders, a burden that I had put on myself ever since I was a little kid. I wish I knew this performance equation when I was going through my teenage years.

What does the equation A × B = Results mean?

The A in the equation is your performance. It is everything that you bring to that very performance that you are in control of. Here are a few examples:

- The talent/skills/experience/knowledge/fitness you possess at that moment in time
- How well rested you are
- Your nutritional status/energy level/hydration
- Your level of commitment to the task in which you are engaged

- The effort and specific focus you bring to the moment of that performance.

The B in the equation are the things that are out of your control, such as:

- What someone else may do
- Rules and regulations
- Umpiring decisions
- Quality of your opposition
- Equipment issues
- The conditions you face
- The match-ups during the game
- Selection and opportunities in a game
- The attitude of the people around you
- The effectiveness and talent of your teammates
- What your competitors choose to do.

I had always believed growing up that A = Results. If I worked hard enough, if I trained my backside off, that I would get the results every single time I played. That's the pressure I put myself under every time I went out to play. I didn't factor in that someone could be better than me on the day. I didn't factor in that I could get a bad umpiring decision or even a favourable umpiring decision. The conditions might not have suited me or they might have suited me perfectly. Sometimes I might have got the results despite not bringing the best version of myself in terms of the A factors, simply because a number of B factors fell my way. If and when I didn't get the results that I was wanting, I simply believed that I wasn't working hard enough. So I would go back to the nets the following week and work even harder, thinking I was closer to guaranteeing my results for the next game.

It wasn't until I really understood the correlation of A and B factors on results, that I thought, 'Oh my gosh, what have I been doing? Why have I been putting so much pressure on myself for so long?'

The A factors

Let's look at the A factors in detail. It's your performance. It's what you bring to that moment in time. It's your talents, skills, your fitness at that moment in time as well. It's your knowledge, your experience, all those sorts of things. It's also your preparation. How well rested you are, your nutrition, your energy levels, whether you're sick or not, or carrying an injury or not. Another important part of this is your level of commitment to that task on the day. Because you could have all the skills and knowledge, you could be really well-rested, you could be hydrated and everything like that. But just at that moment in time you're not fully committed to it. You might have had three great games in a row and in the lead-up you're thinking, 'I don't really care if I miss out today, what about some other guys actually pulling their weight.' Even though you've got all of the other A factors under control, you're not fully committed to that task. You might have a momentary lapse in commitment and effort. You could be fully committed for most of your performance but just not correctly focused for one moment and you make a mistake. This is why you can see some of the most experienced world-class performers sometimes making rookie errors. It's primarily because they just weren't committed enough to that task and were on cruise control instead of being meaningfully engaged in the game right at that moment in time. These are the A factors. It's everything you're in control of.

The B factors

The B factors are the ones that are outside of your control. In cricket or in sport, it's what someone else does, or what your opponent does. Does someone just match up really well against you? Do they push the legal limit on certain things? It's also things like getting a bad umpiring decision or your equipment being faulty. In cricket, your bat might break and you get caught on the fence. You may have to bowl with a wet ball or the crease may be slippery to bowl on. Someone might not care as much and you're the one who's actually gunning for it. In a team sport especially, your success can be dictated by having batters that bat with you and having fielders that want to catch for you. The attitude of people around you, and the effectiveness and talent of your teammates around you can also influence your results. These are the B factors that are out of your control. Another big B factor in cricket is selection. Whether you get selected or not from a subjective selector or coach is also out of your control. And then with this, the opportunities that you get in a game can be dictated by the circumstances of the game. Decisions on when you bat or bowl are B factors that are out of our control. There can be both positive and negative sides to this.

A big B factor that I keep coming back to in cricket is the conditions.

This is something that I had to accept even though I was always working incredibly hard to be able to reduce the impact that these B factors would have. For example, when I was playing the 2019 IPL and I was batting in Chennai, the pitches were not great and spinning a lot. As soon as that happened, it was a battle not to say to myself, 'What the hell am I going to do? I can't score runs in these conditions, I'm really, really going to struggle.'

It's understanding that certain conditions, certain match-ups might well expose your weaknesses. But then it's understanding how to be able to reduce that B factor on the outcome.

These B factors can have two sides. The B factors can be positive as well. The match-up might be an amazing match-up for you. The way a person bowls or bats against you might just suit you down to the ground and you know you can get on top of them, as opposed to having a difficult match-up that will expose your weakness. The conditions can be a positive B factor. The surface might be superb for batting or for your particular type of bowling. Someone could drop a catch while you are batting or they could drop a catch while you are bowling. One day you could play and miss while batting and the next day you could nick the first ball. It is important to understand the influence the B factors can have on the outcome and that you can't control them.

It is very important to note though that the B factors are not cop-outs either. They are not to be used as excuses. It's understanding that in the lead-up to a game, I need to identify what the potential negative B factors might be, so in my planning and preparation I can prepare for those possible scenarios. Then, if a negative B factor comes up in the game, I've worked through possible solutions and I can reduce the impact of the B factor on the outcome, instead of it being something I haven't prepared for and allowing it to have a massive impact on the outcome. The B factors are important to identify and understand as a way to plan and prepare your A factors.

For me, it was a case of realising that I've got to let go of the worry about what might happen and the things I can't control. I've got to understand that it is always A × B = Results.

For me to get the best result that I can, I have to accept that B factors will play a part. It's not actually using that as an excuse to say, 'Oh well I got a bad umpiring decision.' I've got to work on not allowing the umpire the opportunity to make that mistake.

This also changed how I assessed my performances when I reviewed games. Previously, I would beat myself up if I didn't get the result I wanted. I was always technically driven and my assessment after getting out would be completely around technique with my coaches. I would go back and work harder on my technique with my coach in the lead-up to the next game. Coaches always looked at the technical side of things but no coach ever asked me where my mind was during the delivery, or the lead-up to the delivery, or the overs before, the morning of or the lead-up to a game. So my assessment never focused on fixing those things.

But after I understood the performance equation, my self-assessment was very different. My first question was, did I bring my best A's to this performance? What was my preparation like? Could I have done more? How was my mental energy stores in the lead-up to the game and during the performance? And how was my focus during the game? Was it where it needed to be and when it needed to be? And then I would assess what happened and why the result was not what I wanted. What were the negative B's that had an impact on the result? And how could I learn from the negative B factors to take into my preparation in the lead-up to the next game.

After that clinical review, I would move on with no more thoughts. I would especially avoid beating myself up with negative thoughts that were never very productive.

If I look back across all the good days I had throughout my career, there were definitely a lot of little positive B factors that fell my way. Yes, I might have been right at the top of my game, but there were still little B factors always falling my way.

And yes, the best players that I played with or against, some of the world's best-ever cricketers, were subject to the same two factors as the rest of us. These guys definitely brought better A factors into the game, but they still needed smaller B's to go their way. And because they were so well-skilled and equipped, they certainly didn't allow as many negative B's to have a huge impact on the result. There normally weren't too many big negative B's that would impact their results.

KEY TAKEAWAYS

- We don't need to get bent all out of shape when we don't get the results we are wanting, to show that we deeply care about results.

- The only part of the Performance Equation that we can control is the A — exactly what we bring to the performance.

- The B factors are out of our control, and there are positive and negative B's that can influence the results.

- We don't use the negative B factors as an excuse — we use the potential negative B factors in our preparation, in an attempt to limit their influence during our performance.

6

How Mindset Affects Performance

How can I pull myself into the one place that everyone is chasing, 'the zone'?

In 2015, when I was absolutely nowhere mentally, I did a dominant motivators questionnaire. It was a series of questions designed to find out where my mind was right at that point in time. As you can imagine, my scores were skewed very much towards the opposite of a good mindset. Clearly, that was having a huge impact on my performances.

The absolute power of the performance equation is learning that for me to get the best results possible all I needed to do is put all of my mental energy into focusing on the A factors, to control what I could control and bring the best A factors that I possibly could.

You want to stay totally present, be process-driven, focused, and homed in on executing your skills one ball or one moment at a time, and the results will look after themselves.

For a long time it's been popular to speak of 'the zone' – a flow state when you're at your absolute best, totally present throughout, repeating your process over and over again. Time seems to disappear. In a batting sense, you can be four hours into an innings and ask, 'Where did that time go?'

You've simply been in that moment, with a clear and concise mindset, focused on execution, for hours on end. That is what you are chasing. You want to be fully present and focused on A. Everyone wants to find the magical zone. That's how you pull yourself into 'the zone'.

Imagine if everyone in your team understood this really simple process of trying to pull yourself into 'the zone' ball after ball, and a couple of players within the team actually did it in the same game? It would mean a pretty good result in the end just by taking control of what you can control and just doing it ball after ball, or time after time.

What you want to avoid is the focus on outcomes and results. Thoughts like 'I need to score runs today. I need to get a hundred today. It's a flat wicket, I need to make the most of it today' or 'I need to get wickets today. I should be getting wickets on this bowler-friendly pitch.'

You do have to be aware of results though. Imagine you are walking to the top of a mountain. If you are fully focused on every step in front of you and singularly focused on that, you might end up in a different direction to what your goal is. You do need to focus on each step in front of you, to not slip and fall, but you also need to keep glancing at the top of the mountain so you've got an understanding of the direction that you need to go. You need a little bit of awareness that you're headed in the right direction, but a fixation on your destination can lead to not being aware of every step in front of you, and you can slip down the side of a cliff that you did not see. This is really the difference between being aware as to how things are going versus being solely focused on the result.

A mountaintop is actually very important. A great example of this from my own career was in ODI cricket. I was so much better batting second. It took the emphasis away from my own score, which I never thought about, and onto the target. I was glancing at the mountaintop target and then focusing on the steps to get there. Unsurprisingly, I averaged 52 when chasing in ODI cricket, compared to just under 34 when batting first.

The things you want to avoid coming into your mind are, of course, the B factors. Something that might come up is the fear of failure. If you think about when you've been at your absolute best, you've got absolutely no fear of making a mistake and the B factors don't enter your mind whatsoever.

With the new understanding of the control you have over your conscious mind, as soon as you start to hear the internal dialogue move towards the B factors, the fear of getting out, the results, you need to grab a hold of that conversation and redirect that script immediately back onto the execution part, the process.

THINKING IN THE ZONE

WHAT THEY FOCUS ON...	EXECUTION ("A") %	"RESULTS" %	AVOID FAILURE ("B") %
IN GENERAL	55 – 65%	30 – 35%	5 – 15%
"IN THE ZONE"	90 – 95%	5 – 10%	0%

When I did the dominant motivators questionnaire initially, when I was struggling mentally, my focus on A, the execution, was only 40 per cent.

My results focus was extremely high at 50 per cent and my fear of failure focus was 10 per cent!

I was so obsessed with the results because results were so bloody important to me and I wasn't getting the results that I knew I should have been getting with all of the skills that I had developed over my career. And my fear of failure had a lot to do with the fear of what might happen to me when I was facing the fast bowlers after that tragic event the year or so before.

As soon as I understood that to be at my best, I just needed to pull myself back to my A and just be focused on the process and repeat that over and over again, I finally had an understanding of how to pull myself into the zone, instead of hoping the seas parted and I fell into the zone.

I definitely did have quite a few days up until that point where I had been in the zone, that holy grail of performance. But it was the circumstances around me that made me fall into the right headspace, to be singularly focused on the A's, the process, and just continue to do it until the day was done.

Normally these circumstances were around proving someone wrong or getting into the battle on the field, which sharpened my focus to the moment and repeating it over and over again. It certainly wasn't me having the control to pull myself into that headspace.

When you're in the zone, 90–95 per cent of your focus is on 'What do I need to do right now?' and repeating that thought over and over again. There is an awareness of the results as we've discussed, but there's no fixation or worry about the results. It's not the 50 per cent focus that I had. And there is never, ever any fear of failure whatsoever. There is no voice saying 'Don't play that shot because I might get out' or 'Don't bowl that ball because I might get hammered.'

This idea that if I'm aware of and can control my internal dialogue, I can redirect the script to where it needs to be at a certain moment in time, and I can repeat this process over and over again, changed things in a huge way for me.

This thinking can apply to all aspects of life. A lot of people are wasting a lot of mental capacity by focusing 30–35 per cent on results and 5–15 per cent on the fear of failure, when just about all of your mental processing needs to be redirected onto execution, and repeated time after time, moment after moment, ball after ball. A simple shift can get you back towards your best.

There are three examples I can give you about how shifting your mindset to the process can produce the results that you want.

Ricky Ponting explained in *Lessons Learnt with the Greats* that he used to religiously ask the umpire how many balls were left in the over. He always knew when there were two balls left. He did this to stay totally focused and driven to get through to the end of each over because his dad told him as a youngster that it was criminal if he got out the last two balls of an over.

I knew how many balls were gone. Every time I knew there were four balls gone. But I still had to ask how many were left, because then I wasn't going to get out in those last couple of balls.

Every single over I ever batted with Ricky, and some of the biggest partnerships of my career were batting with Ricky, he would ask how many balls were left in the over and he always knew it was two, but it was his cue to stay totally present on just getting to the end of the over. He would do this over and over again.

Another example is from Matthew Hayden. He talked about not looking at the scoreboard. In my first ever Test match as a part of the Test squad in South Africa 2002, he was a few runs away from his hundred and then when he got the runs, there was an obvious delay between him hitting those runs and the time he celebrated. Why? Because he had an idea he was close to a hundred, as he had been out there for quite a while and the crowd was getting louder, but he never looked at the scoreboard. He explained the reasons why.

If you're scoreboard watching, it takes forever to get to 10 runs, forever, it's a lifetime. And the chances are that you probably won't get there because that's pressure. So by just staying so singular, and it's a really difficult thing to do, it doesn't matter whether you're on nought or getting close to 100. You kind of know when you're getting close to milestones. But also beyond those milestone figures, it is the possibility of what hasn't been done before is the thing that I found most restrictive about watching the scoreboard. Because if you're looking at the scoreboard, you're not thinking of the moment, you're not entertaining the possibilities of the future. And it seems like such a simple thought process.

This is how mentally tough and process driven he was. He had no care at all about the outcome, how many runs he was on, it was all about staying present and just reacting to the ball over and over again and the scoreboard would look after itself. Now this takes a lot of mental discipline.

An example of how I did this myself, and it's an example I'll keep referring to in this book, is the 2018 IPL Final while playing for Chennai Super Kings against Sunrisers Hyderabad. I was 0 off 10 at one point chasing 179. But I didn't focus on the pressure of the scoreboard. I kept pulling myself back into the present, on my technical and mental checklists and going through those every ball. I stayed totally present for every ball. The end result was 117 not out and victory. I'll explain in more detail how I went about it later on.

The fundamental truth to the performance equation

For this equation to be true we need to understand one key point. If I can't control B, which I can't because they are factors out of my control, that means I can't control Results.

The one question that I never deeply thought about was: if I bring the best version of myself to a performance, does this guarantee that I am going to get the results that I want? Well, the answer is no. Because there are these B factors that can get in the way, and they can have a significant impact on the outcome. But throughout my teenage years and through my 20s, I didn't have this perspective at all. I just believed that I wasn't working hard enough, so I would punish myself by going back to the nets after the game to work harder. Because, in my mind, this was the reason why I wasn't getting the results I was looking for every time.

If we can't control the results, then why are we always so fixated on them? The only thing that we can control is the A factors, so this is the only thing that we need to focus on. Yes, results are very important to all of us. Everyone wants to be as successful as possible. But when it is all boiled down, for me to get the best results possible, all I can do is focus on the A's and bring the best A's that I possibly can. Because if I am in control of this and just do this ball after ball, then the result will be the best it can be, not knowing what the B factors are going to be during that performance.

There are two powerful questions that have to be asked. When has worrying about the result ever made the result better, or more likely? And, when has worrying about failure made failure less likely? Both answers are *Never*. So why do we waste so much mental energy and time worrying about the result, or worrying about failing, when this has no impact on whether the results are going to be better or not? This was so profound for me.

For this equation to be fundamentally true, then the only thing that we are in control of is A. And this equation is fundamentally true. Once you deeply believe this to be true, your world will be very different in a great way and this realisation will help you to crush any anxiety you might have.

KEY TAKEAWAYS

- When I am at my absolute best, I have 0 per cent fear of failure in my mind.
- To pull yourself into the zone, 90–95 per cent of your mental processing needs to be on the A factors, with

5–10 per cent having an awareness on the result to ensure you are on the right path.

- When has worrying about the result made the result better? And when has worrying about failing ever made failure less likely? NEVER.

7

Team Environment

What does a high-performing team environment really look like?

Sometimes team, work, study or school environments can drag you into focusing on results too much, rather than the A factors and the execution of the A factors, the things you are in control of.

There are environments where the leaders talk about how big this game is, how important this game is, and say, 'If we lose this game, we are out.' I have been in plenty of these team environments. There are also environments where leaders talk about how performance in this game will dictate selection, and that underperformance might lead to players getting dropped. I have heard from leaders of a number of teams that I have played in say things like, 'Spots are up for grabs in the game' or 'If you don't perform you will get dropped.'

So guess what people are thinking in those environments? 'Don't lose. I really need to perform today. I need to score runs. We need to win. Don't get out. Don't bowl badly. Don't stuff up otherwise I might be gone.' All of these focus on results and fear of failure.

These environments can work for a shorter period of time where fear of failure can drive individuals to be ready to lock in for one very important game. But these environments are not sustainable at all, as stress and anxiety builds up to a point where the whole team implodes, and I have been a part of these environments on a few occasions too. The telltale signs are that everyone starts to only play for themselves, for their individual spots, and as long as they do enough to get picked for the next game, they are happy. This always leads to an incredibly toxic team environment where the enjoyment factor of playing the game that you love evaporates and it turns into every person for themselves. We should be doing all that we can to do the opposite of this, as the best and most successful team environments always have a fun and enjoyable aspect to them as a very important undercurrent to all that they do.

Other environments I have been a part of are ones where there is a clear focus on the process and leaders ask the players to just bring the best version of themselves every time and to do it over and over again. They reiterate that if we all do this, we give ourselves the best chance of coming out on top. This is exactly what a championship mindset looks like!

This is what made Ricky Ponting such a good captain. He always said to the team in the lead-up to big games that the team whose individuals do the basics better and for longer will be the team that will come out on top. It focused our minds on the process, on doing the basics, controlling the A factors.

Paddy Upton for Rajasthan Royals built a process-driven environment that took all of the anxiety and stress out of a very pressurised tournament where performance and results were so important. The other team environment where this was done incredibly well was at Chennai Super Kings in the IPL under captain MS Dhoni and coach Stephen Fleming. I never heard either of them say, 'We need to win this game today', or 'If you don't score runs today or take wickets, you will be getting dropped.'

My second year with CSK really stuck with me. There was no chopping and changing in selection. In other teams I had been with, players were turned over constantly. If a player didn't perform for a couple of games, selectors would think he wasn't good enough and would replace him immediately. This meant that everyone started looking over their shoulders and thinking, 'Gosh, if I don't perform in a couple of games, then I could be gone too.'

No matter who we are, we are always going to have times in our lives where we are in a 'results-focused' environment. By understanding the mental skills framework in this book, we know that this is the opposite of where we want to be mentally for us to be at our best, both individually and collectively. We need to listen to what is being said by the leaders in this environment and we need to redirect their words ourselves to say, 'I am not going to let their results focus influence the correct mindset I need for me to be at my best.' This can be much easier said than done when players are being chopped and changed from one game to the next without any rhyme or reason, apart from someone not performing in one game. But understanding this will be a powerful tool for you to use throughout your life to ensure a negative environment doesn't infiltrate your thinking and pull you out of your high-performance mindset.

I've been a victim of a negative team environment. After the retirement of Ricky Ponting and Mike Hussey, the Australian team drifted significantly. Pressure to perform began to affect confidence and consistency. Players, myself included, began to look over our shoulders. I didn't have knowledge of the mental skills I needed to redirect my thoughts to the right things at the right times to consistently bring the best version of myself into every performance, instead of being overcome with fear of failure and overwhelmed by a need for results, which saw my performances go downhill throughout that time. And this was all at a time where I was in my prime, performing really well in the IPL in an incredibly enjoyable, process-driven team environment. But as soon as I went back into this other environment, my kryptonite, my performances started to tank again and the enjoyment factor of playing the game that I loved evaporated very quickly.

My last three months with the Australia T20 team from early January 2016 through to the T20 World Cup in India was another example of one of those environments. We played India in a three-match T20 International series, where the selectors picked a really big squad and chopped and changed the team significantly from game to game, and then this flowed onto a T20 series in South Africa before we headed to India for the T20 World Cup. The conversations and actions around the group from the leaders, that being the coach, captain, selectors, had consistent messaging like, 'All spots are up for grabs if you want to play in the T20 World Cup' and 'You need to perform in this game as you might only have one opportunity to press your claim.'

As soon as I heard and saw this, I immediately acknowledged in my own mind what this ridiculous situation was creating.

This time I opted out. I knew the importance of preparation and focus, of distinguishing between A and B factors. The result was that I bowled as well as I had in T20 cricket for Australia, played one of the games of my life at the SCG as captain, and retired at the end of the T20 World Cup as the No.1 T20I all-rounder in the world.

Surprise surprise, we lost to India in the quarter final knock-out game. We left a few runs on the table and didn't execute that well with the ball against an Indian team that had barely changed their XI from the first game that we played against them during the series in Australia, three months before.

But the attitudes I saw in that T20 World Cup are everywhere. I saw it recently in a game of junior cricket. The result of the match was important as a place in the grand final was riding on it. A number of the parents had really built this game up as being a knock-out game and had stressed to the kids how important it was to win to make the final. Then one of the calmest kids in the team went out to bat with two overs to go and one of the parents said, 'Don't get out, otherwise we will lose' as he walked out to bat. And guess what happened. This poor young kid ended up getting out, and because of all of the build-up of importance for this game by the parents and kids around him, the calmest child on the field lost the plot, throwing his gear everywhere in disappointment because he felt he'd let the team down. It was so sad to see and something that should never happen if the parents around the team simply understood the fundamentals of how to create the optimal environment. Reinforcement of the correct mindset would then filter down to all of the young kids.

It is so easy to allow the 'live or die by results' environment to infiltrate your mindset and start to corrupt it. It is easy to start to move your thinking to fear of failure and how important it is to perform and get results. But by understanding all of the mental skills in this book, you will be armed with all that you need to be mentally tough enough to create a super strong cocoon around yourself, to just direct your thoughts to continually creating your optimal mental environment to bring the best version of you, no matter what team environment you are in.

We need to do all that we can in our power to help create the best team environment possible, so that individuals don't have to feel like they are rebelling against the team leadership just to stay process-driven, to bring their best A game possible, game in game out. I'm convinced that more and more teams should be open to allowing players to manage their own mental and physical preparation. Everyone is different; everyone comes to know what best suits them; just as a lot of cricket is individual, so should a lot of the preparation be too. Understanding this will create so many more high-performing team environments, high-performing individuals and most importantly, much more enjoyable team environments too, so that we never lose the fun and joy that we get playing the game that we love.

KEY TAKEAWAYS

- Understand the power of leaders in a group to create the highest-performing team environment.
- Building up how important a game is, or that selection is on the line if you don't perform, creates a high-stress team environment that leads to a 'every person for themselves' mentality.
- Messages and actions of the leaders to keep everyone process-driven and bringing the best version of themselves to give themselves the best chance of falling on the right side of the result creates a high-performing team environment that is a lot more fun to be a part of.

8

Communication and the Power of It

How important are the words that we use to getting our message across?

When we are trying to create the best team environment possible, one of the really important components of this is communication and how our messages are conveyed and received by the other person.

One of the most renowned behavioural psychologists, Dr Albert Mehrabian, did extensive research on communication and the powers of verbal versus non-verbal communication. His research resulted in the 7-38-55 Rule, which absolutely fascinated me. What was revealed was that seven per cent of your communication is done through the words that you use, 38 per cent of your communication is through your tone of voice and 55 per cent of any communication is through your body language. This really hit home to me, as I was always someone who was as careful as possible to use the right words every time that I was communicating with someone within a team environment. But Mehrabian's research shows that the non-verbal aspect of communication is so much more important, in terms of your tone of voice and your body language that goes with it. Those two elements make up 93 per cent of how your communication is received.

So what does this mean in a team environment? It means we have to be very careful of how we say what we're saying, as tone of voice and body language have the most influence in any communication that we have.

Finally, while I am on the topic of communication within a team environment, especially when there is potentially a language or cultural hurdle, it is so important to ensure that the message you think you are conveying and the message that the other person is receiving are the same. Every time you are having a really important conversation with someone, you need to ask the person to repeat your message back to you, to ensure that the message was received as you intended it. Things can be unintentionally lost in translation. It is important that everyone is always on the same page. So we need to make sure that the message that we are trying to convey is received as intended by the person listening.

KEY TAKEAWAYS

- Tone of voice and body language make up 93 per cent of your communication with others.
- When you have an important message to deliver, ensure that the receiver of the message has received it as intended. You only know this by asking for this person to repeat back to you what has been said.

9

The Demon of Expectation

How can a goal or expectation of a result have a significant impact on the outcome?

The demon of expectation is a beast. Growing up in cricket, the demon of expectation for me was that to be a great batter you needed to score hundreds. All of the best batters scored hundreds. All through my teenage years, it was drummed into me. All of my expectations were around needing to score hundreds, and that flowed on into my Test career. When you have that outcome in your mind, as you get closer to the milestone, you start to pay more attention to it and stop focusing on the A factors, the process of execution that got you there.

And this was a pattern that started for me as a kid, all the way through my teenage years and then into my international career as well. The following example shows the same patterns of thinking that most often entered my mind ever since I can remember.

It was during a Test match in the 2010–11 Ashes series in Perth. I was batting really well, and I was on 95. It was a beautiful wicket to bat on and the ball was coming on so nicely as it normally does at the WACA. At this very moment in time I started to think, 'Wow, this is going to be my first Ashes Test hundred, how am I going to celebrate? How amazing is this going to feel? What am I going to do?'

My mind moved to the outcome, to this expectation that I had always set for myself. 'I'm going well. I'm nearly there. I am so close to achieving one of the dreams that I have had since I was a kid. How am I going to get to a hundred? With a six or a boundary or just get five singles?' Whereas up until this moment, I had not been thinking about how I was going to score runs. I was just in the moment, trusting my instincts with aggressive intent, ball after ball. This mindset was what had got me to 95.

I should have been thinking, 'What do I need to do right now? And what do I need to keep doing to be able to give myself the best chance of getting there?' I didn't know how to grab hold of that mental script that had started to come in, thanks to that little bird on my shoulder, and say, 'Be quiet!', and pull myself back into the exact same mindset that had worked so well up to that point.

I ended up getting out LBW to Chris Tremlett. The ball angled into middle stump and I just missed a straight one. My mind had moved forward to the future and the outcome, instead of just staying present in the execution mode and doing that over and over again, and what would be would be.

Where the stress and anxiety lie is in the gap between where we are currently and what our expectations are. If we have started off poorly, then our mind shifts to the gap between where we are and where we need to get to. This normally causes a large amount of worry, stress and anxiety and shifts our minds away from being in the present, totally focused and process driven. Instead we start singularly focusing on the result and how big this gap is. And this means that our ability to close the gap by moving back onto execution has stopped.

Yes, we all set goals. I had always dreamed of an Ashes hundred. In business, for example, everyone has set targets. Most of the time, everyone is setting targets or goals that they must achieve to get bonuses or a promotion, for example. Or to achieve high marks in exams or assignments.

But all this does is build up this anxiety and stress and focus on results. And particularly if you're not on target, then everyone starts to freak out. But there might be B factors at play. You might be bringing the best A game that you can and the whole group might be bringing the best A version of themselves.

But there might be some things that are out of their control, which are having a significant impact on the results. But everyone starts to worry about the results. They start worrying about losing their job or having their salary reduced.

The better way to think of targets, expectations, or goals, is to use them as a guide. They are like the mountaintop in the distance, only to be glanced at, because the ability to achieve them can change when B factors influence things that are out of your control. It's a fine line between results-driven and results-focused. The stress and worry of being results-focused has a huge impact on your ability to achieve your desired outcomes, and even your health. Results-driven, on the other hand, is being desperate and very disciplined to do all you can to get the best results possible, which is pulling yourself back to your best A's.

Interestingly, when I was having all those troubles getting out in the 90s, I talked to Michael Clarke about it. He said, 'My goal is actually 150, it's not 100. So, when I'm in the 90s I don't care because my goal is to get 150, not 100.' That's why he hardly ever got out in the 90s. He just cruised through it. I couldn't believe how easy he made it look. But he said, 'My goal is way above that so that I'm just going to continue to focus on what I'm doing.'

KEY TAKEAWAYS

- The demon of expectation pulls your mind into how you are doing and the gap between where you are and where you want to be instead of what you need to do right now to stay on task.
- Goals are important to push yourself but a fixation on achieving them no matter what is disastrous.
- We can be results-driven but not results-focused — a very important difference.

10

Skill of Focus

How do I focus more effectively and when I lose my focus, how do I regain it quickly?

I want to put you through a really simple test. It's designed to test how good your focus is. Below is a grid with 100 numbers on it. Before you start, so you don't cheat, place a piece of paper over the grid so you can't see it. All you need is a stopwatch or a timer on your phone and a pen or pencil. Set the timer at 60 seconds. The numbers in the grid start at 00 and go all the way to 99, randomly distributed throughout this grid of 100 boxes. Once you start the timer, remove the paper and work through finding the numbers in order. You need to find 00, draw a line through it, then find 01, cross it off, 02, 03, and so on up into the 40s or 50s, in sequence. It's not seeing the number or two in front of the number you are looking for and crossing them off. The numbers have to be crossed off in ascending order, starting at 00. You need to be as fast as you can with this within the 60 seconds to get as far into the grid as possible.

Before you start I will give you one simple tip to help you to be as fast as you possibly can. You need to pull your focus back, open up the lens a bit. If you are looking for the number 44 for example, you need to view it like you've got an overhead projector over the top of the grid. And all you need do is project the number 44, and hover it above the page in your mind. You will be surprised how it will just pop out at you. If you start going up and down the grid and then across the rows looking for 44 you will end up being very slow.

Are you ready? Set the timer. And once you hit start, remove the piece of paper covering the grid and have a go.

Grid A

Final Score:

40	86	59	99	13	98	25	03	78	43
04	27	48	39	84	58	92	96	76	41
71	97	45	95	20	33	29	87	09	89
94	08	49	00	54	93	44	10	75	30
17	36	24	60	91	26	53	85	67	79
73	61	12	69	21	66	77	16	01	31
35	02	72	28	46	83	18	22	88	56
63	15	90	14	37	55	62	42	32	68
82	19	81	50	38	64	05	80	11	57
06	34	23	70	52	07	74	65	47	51

How did you go? If you got under 20 that's not a great result. You should be aiming for the 40s and 50s.

Let's try again with Grid B. Start the stopwatch again.

Grid B

Final Score:

47	69	03	54	66	24	99	89	63	34
14	97	75	96	15	53	79	06	16	94
20	46	88	29	93	91	85	33	78	65
83	64	11	52	19	42	12	87	21	48
04	98	35	92	74	10	81	30	32	00
95	39	62	07	37	70	90	71	59	72
28	57	43	51	27	84	05	38	77	13
86	01	76	22	82	67	02	31	25	60
41	73	44	40	17	56	80	68	08	49
23	61	09	45	36	58	18	50	55	26

How did you go? Did your focus shift from where it needs to be, hovering above the page, to narrowly chasing the number by snaking up and down in the rows in the grid? Did you ever doubt the number was actually there? If you did, you are not alone. I did several times when I first did this exercise. Did you look at the stopwatch at all? Did you feel the time pressure? One minute is a very short space of time. Did you also feel the pressure of expectation between Grid A and Grid B after I mentioned that you should be aiming for 40 or 50?

Well, this was part of the exercise. The actual average for people doing this exercise is between 10 and 12 in 60 seconds. This average includes highly focused people like special forces personnel, racing car drivers, and other cricketers, who would say they are mentally tough and very much in control of their mind. If you beat that you did really well, and even if you only got to the average that is still an excellent result. If you fell short of the average, don't worry, a lot of people do. Part of the reason why I told you to get a number in the 40s and 50s was to highlight the demon of expectation – thinking about how you are doing instead of being focused on what you are doing.

It is a great way to be able to challenge yourself and grow your skill of focus. You can start to learn how your mind works under that pressure and how even in a minute your focus of attention shifts away from where it really needs to be, to get through the grid as fast as you can.

When I first did it, I only got to number 08 or 09. But the more I practised it the better I got. I was able to hover the number above the page and scan it broadly and the number jumped out at me. The best I ever got was in the mid-20s, when I was singularly focused on the right thing. You can try this grid again in a number of different ways to improve your focus. You can start at 20 or 30 or 50 or 70 so you don't learn the pattern. You can also do it for 3 or 5 minutes as well, to really test out your skill of focus over a longer period of time.

By doing this grid exercise in many different ways, it means that you are able to develop and grow your skill of focus without even going to the nets or playing a game of cricket. The skill of focus is a skill in itself, which means we can work on it and get better at it by training the mental muscle to keep pulling ourselves back to the present by having one thought on the number hovering above the page and continually redirecting our mind back to this one thought over and over again. This is the exact skill you need to develop and get better at, having one thought on what you need right now to execute your skill to the best of your ability. Just keep listening in to where your mind is focusing, and continually redirect it back to the right thing at the right time.

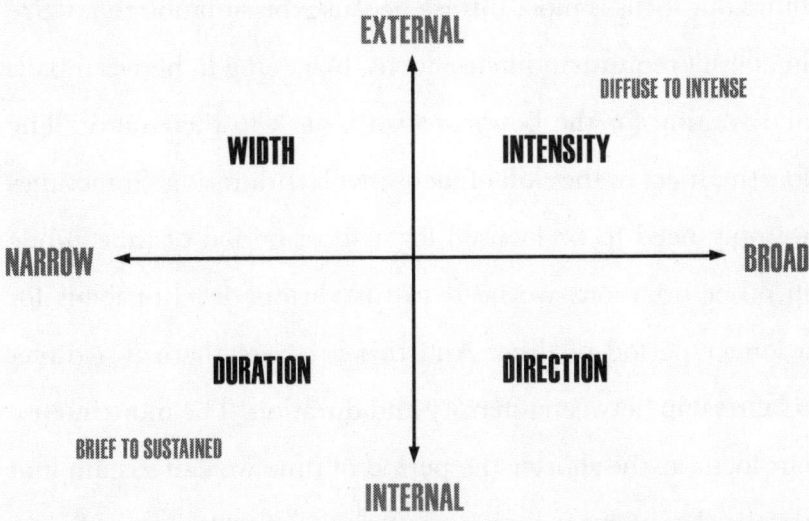

There are a number of different facets to the skill of focus that are really important to understand. The first is width. Your focus can be either broad or narrow. A broad focus in cricketing terms would be your general awareness and relaxed state in between balls. A narrow focus would be watching the ball while batting or fielding or focusing on your target while bowling or throwing.

Then there is the direction of your focus. Is it external? Am I interacting with my environment around me or is it internal? Am I inside my own head working through something?

The third factor is the intensity of your focus. Sometimes our focus of attention is intense because we are about to face the ball coming down or we are running in to bowl. While at other times our focus is more diffuse because the situation that we're in doesn't require an intense focus, like being in between balls and waiting for the bowler to walk back to their mark. The fourth aspect in the skill of focus involves duration. Sometimes we only need to be focused for a short period of time, while in other situations we need to sustain our level of focus for a longer period of time. And this is where there is a direct relationship between intensity and duration. The more intense our focus is, the shorter the period of time we can sustain it at that level of intensity without suffering mental fatigue or 'brain fade'. Conversely, if we only need to be generally aware and are chilling, we can sustain that level for a much longer period of time.

That is the reason why special forces soldiers and air traffic controllers, for example, work short shifts. They don't get the opportunity to switch off their intensity during operations, as they need to be mentally switched on right there and then just in case they have to take action, which is why they have to work in shifts. Otherwise, mental fatigue will set in and they could make a mistake when everything is on the line.

It's important to understand that the skill of focus is not about being really good at one of these in particular, it is about being able to shift between the various facets as you need them. In a cricketing sense, when do I need to be narrowly and intensely focused? When the ball is about to be bowled. But outside of that, I need to be broadly focused with my brain on neutral so I'm not burning any extra mental energy. I may still need to be thinking of the game and strategy but I can do that from a broad and less intense focused state.

When do I need to be externally focused? Again, when the ball is being bowled. But when I'm at the non-striker's or walking back to my mark or in the field in between balls, I can be internally focused on what I need to do next.

I also need to understand when to be intense and when to be relaxed. Cricket is a long game. Even T20 cricket takes over three hours. I need to have enough mental energy throughout that time period so that I can access all of my skills when I really need them. I know if I am tired and mentally fatigued then my ability to execute my skills to the best of my ability, to have full control over my A factors, is going to be reduced.

I had no understanding of the skill of focus during my Test career.

And I didn't know there was a skill in using my focus correctly.

I had heard people talk about the need to switch on and off in between balls, as it was impossible to concentrate for a whole day of Test cricket. But no one had ever put it in simple, layman's terms for me to understand that your brain is very much like a muscle: once you run out of energy, your performance will fall away sharply.

The only way for me to understand what component of the skill of focus that I need at any moment in time is to be totally present. Which aspect do I need right now? In between balls, I need to pull back and be broadly focused, on neutral. When the bowler is running in, I need to be narrowly focused, zeroing in on the ball.

I wish I had known about the skill of focus earlier and had this mental routine in between every ball that I bowled and faced as a batter. I was narrowly and intensely focused so regularly during my Test career when I certainly didn't need to be, because I was so desperate for the results I was dreaming of.

KEY TAKEAWAYS

- The skill of focus is something that we can work on and get better at.
- We don't need to be better at one facet of the skill of focus, we just need to know which one we need at a particular moment in time.
- The only way we know which facet we need in the moment is by being totally present.

11

The Brain is Like a Muscle

How much impact does brain fatigue have on my performances?

When you are mentally fatigued your neural pathways get clogged. Your decision-making and your execution of your skills grow sluggish. You know those days where you're thinking of a word that you know but it just won't come to you? This is to do with mental fatigue. There are other days when your decision-making is like a superhighway. It is instant and decisive. This amount of mental energy is what we are chasing every time we go out to play.

When our mental energy stores are high, we find it very easy to tap into our unconscious mind decision-making process – the 'gut feel' – which is so powerful. We find it really easy to pull ourselves back on task when our mind starts to wander a little.

But when we are mentally fatigued, we are suppressing our ability to tap into our gut feel. One of the biggest issues is that we are very easily distracted and find it hard to keep pulling ourselves back to being totally present and being correctly focused on the execution of our skill.

There are two elements to conserving mental energy; one is during the game and one is in the lead-up to the game.

During my international career two of my teammates, Glenn McGrath, Australia's greatest ever fast bowler, and Michael Clarke, one of the best batters of his generation, used to use a simple mental technique to put their minds on neutral during the game. They discovered that they were at their best when they were singing a song in their head.

I never understood why they did it, and they didn't really explain why they did it, apart from both saying they knew it worked really well for them to concentrate for longer periods of time with ease.

Once I came to understand why this technique worked so well for them, I couldn't believe how simple and how unbelievably effective it was. The theory is that your brain is like a muscle, and it only has a certain amount of energy every day. You regenerate it with sleep and meditation. But in cricket, when we spend hours out on the field, we need to place our minds on neutral whenever we can to limit the mental energy we burn and conserve it for when we need to access all of our technical skills. This is exactly what having a song in your head does. It puts one thought in your mind, which is what meditation is in very simple terms. That was why having a song in my head late in my career was so powerful for me. It forced me to have a broad focus in between balls. It put my brain on neutral and I was hardly burning any energy. It was a really simple technique to switch my mind to a broad focus. It helped me sustain my ability to shift focus from narrow to broad, internal to external, intense to diffuse for longer periods of time.

Other players I have spoken to have used their breathing as their focusing technique. That's one way of just pulling themselves back to the present. They just focus on their breathing in between balls. Focusing on breathing is a key part of meditation and helps put your mind on neutral.

The other technique that I was told about came from one of the all-time greats Sir Viv Richards. I was lucky enough to have the West Indies legend as the very first guest on my podcast and he spoke about why he chewed gum. It was part of his iconic image as a cricketer. He took on some of the fastest and best bowlers of all-time wearing just a cap and chewing his gum. But it was also a mental technique he used as he explained below.

It calmed me down a little bit, chewing this gum. It's a certain kind of rhythm as well. The bowler would be going back to his mark. I'm tapping [my bat], I'm chewing, everything worked in sequence.

That was my companion at that time. I'd done away with a mouth piece [for protection] and decided my chewing gum was worth much more in terms of how I wanted to feel as an individual.

Many current players use chewing gum to bring themselves back to the present, to put their mind on neutral and conserve their mental energy.

Conserving your mental energy during the game is so important. But conserving it pre-game is absolutely vital.

As careful as we are with our physical preparation, to be as fresh and as well hydrated as we possibly can to avoid going into the game physically fatigued, we need to be as diligent with our mental preparation too, so that we are going into the game with as much mental energy as possible. To access all of our technical skills and knowledge, we need to be as physically and as mentally fresh as possible and our batteries fully charged.

All of my Test cricket took place prior to me understanding this information. In Test matches, I was the king of burning mental energy. I didn't understand the concept that the brain was like a muscle. I only had a certain amount of energy per day and I was ploughing through it.

I used to let my mind chatter run wild in the lead-up to big games during my international career, especially around Ashes series and World Cup games. Three days out from a Test match I would be walking down to get a coffee and a little voice would be chatting about how I need to score runs, what the bowlers might do, what would happen if I failed. I had no strategies to deal with it. I would wear myself out with worry and my unconscious mind would start taking those cues too.

On the morning of the game, I would wake up and the first thing I would think about was that today had to be my day. That I needed to really concentrate hard today and how important today was for me and my country. This would just go on and on as I was walking out to bat, at the non-striker's end, telling myself how I needed to make this my day and switch on, and the same when I was facing as the bowler was running in and in between balls.

Surprisingly, a lot of the time I would get to 30, 40, or 50 without many problems. I actually made 34 scores between 30 and 59 in Test cricket from 109 innings. But I would then get out playing a false stroke through not having enough energy in my mind and body for that ball, and before I knew it I was sitting back in the dressing room beating myself up about how mentally soft I was. The next step I would go through was to sit down with the coaches and look at the footage of how I got out and work through the technical issues before my next innings. But I never worked on the mental side. This exact cycle was repeated throughout my whole career up until I was 34. When I made an error I always assessed it technically. I never asked the question, and a coach never asked, where was your mind during that ball? Where was your mind in the lead-up to that ball? Where was your mind before the day's play and in the lead-up to the game starting? These questions were never asked, so I never asked them of myself!

I developed a routine in the last four years of my career of setting aside 45 minutes of time prior to leaving for a game. That time was used to do some conscious and unconscious mind preparation. Any time a single thought about the game popped into my head prior to those 45 minutes, I would exercise the control that I had over my conscious mind and redirect these thoughts immediately as I knew I had put time aside to work through it all.

I used those 45 minutes to consciously watch footage of the opposition to work through my game plan, and write down notes. It was a conscious, deliberate process, to put information in my unconscious mind about batting and bowling plans. I'd write in my diary to reinforce my mental and technical cues. At the age of 16, the sports psychologist that I worked with at Queensland Cricket talked about the importance of writing in a diary as a way to finalise your thoughts, instead of letting your thoughts continue to swirl around in your mind. So from that day onwards, I always wrote in a diary before every match that I played until my very last match with CSK as a 39-year-old. I would also watch video footage of me playing at my absolute best for technical and mental reinforcement. Visualisation and imagery are such powerful tools to tap into and I will talk about them in more detail later on. And then I would do a 20-minute meditation. Even in that 45 minutes, I'd burn energy by working through the game plan and watching footage, but then I'd meditate to try and regenerate as much of that mental energy as I could from that preparation time, as well as from my day in the lead-up to that time.

By locking off those 45 minutes pre-game, I was able to conserve so much more mental energy compared to previously burning through it relentlessly with endless mind chatter and unproductive, internal negative thoughts. I will detail my routine further when we start to define the ACT Model.

I used some of these mental energy conservation techniques during my captaincy as well. I can give you an example of what I was like before I used this technique and what I was like after I employed it.

Initially, when I captained the Rajasthan Royals in the 2014 IPL, I would be mentally fried after a big game and especially after back-to-back games. At the time, I was batting in the top four, and often opening the batting. I was also bowling two of the six crucial powerplay overs and then two of the last five overs of an innings, as well as deciding who should bowl when and who should field where. I was also incredibly structured as a captain. I had our bowling innings mapped out with our team analyst before the game and rarely wavered from it. I would overthink situations but rarely wavered from the plan, even if things had changed a little bit and the plan wasn't right for that exact moment.

I had no idea about how to go with the flow of the game, to make the best decisions possible at the right times, and also how to conserve as much mental energy as I could. I didn't know what my mental environment needed to be for me to access all of my skills and knowledge.

This mental fatigue would also affect my decision-making ability as a captain, and while I was batting or bowling. I had days where I just couldn't think of the right ball to bowl or the right bowling change to make because I was so mentally fatigued.

The main technique that I used to overcome this mental exhaustion while trying to make the right decisions was to trust my gut feel. The way I tapped into this was jamming a song into my head so that my mind was on neutral, to create the mental space that I needed for the right decision to pop up from my unconscious mind, every ball.

This was me tapping into the decision-making power of the unconscious mind. Even if I couldn't feel something right there and then, I would leave it as late as I possibly could to allow the feeling to come.

Then if it didn't, which wouldn't happen very often, I would have to decide with my conscious mind. This decision-making technique was superefficient and meant that I wasn't burning unnecessary mental energy by trying to calculate the right decision with my conscious mind by working through countless scenarios and then coming up with the answer.

Fortunately, it is never too late to learn and I was able to rectify these mistakes during the last four years of my T20 career.

In my second coming in 2016, I was able to test these techniques out on the biggest stage. In the third T20 International against India that summer at the Sydney Cricket Ground, I captained Australia for the first time in that format and was again opening the batting and bowling four of the most important overs.

In that game, I used the song in my head to perfection and could not believe the results. I finished the game quite physically fatigued, but mentally I felt like I could have played a few more games back-to-back.

I scored 124 not out from 71 balls, batting the whole innings, and then bowled four overs and took 1 for 30. I bowled one over in the powerplay and two of the last four overs, including the second last over of the match where I conceded just five runs. I did all this while captaining the team. What an obvious contrast it was compared to the previous times when I had no mental energy conservation techniques and I just burned through all that I had in no time at all. Where had these very simple techniques been all of my life?!

I ended up using these techniques with great success in the twilight of my career, but imagine if I knew these techniques as a 16-year-old! I have no doubt in my mind, my Test career runs total and average would have been quite a bit better.

In my very first stint as a coach with the Delhi Capitals, I realised that one of the biggest issues in world cricket right now, that is causing issues for the majority of cricketers, is their ability to conserve their mental energy until the time that they need it most to perform at their best. Browsing social media regularly and playing computer games are great ways to burn through your mental energy unnecessarily. I saw people burning mental energy the way I had. It was crippling.

How we can deplete our mental energy

Ever since I finally understood the very important concept of mental energy and how important it is for me to bring the best that I have to every performance, I have always been super aware of where and when I am using my mental energy in the lead-up to a game. If I want my neural pathways to be superhighways, in order to have my best sharp and precise decision-making during a game, and my best muscle memory skills execution, I need as much mental energy as I possibly can.

After 2015, I never wanted brain fatigue to be my downfall again. I wanted to access all of the skills that I had inside of me, and ensure that I was engaged in the game for every ball. I wanted my conscious mind to not be distracted easily, and have the mental energy to stop the little birdie on my shoulder in its tracks and redirect my thoughts to the right thing at the right time. I also wanted to tap into the power of the unconscious mind for my decision-making during the game. I was desperate to tap into my 'gut feel', as this was when I was making my best decisions and making the most of all of my cricket experiences throughout my life.

Finally, I didn't want to be walking off again after getting out because of mental fatigue, which happened to me so many times, especially during my Test career.

Here are a few ways that I used to burn through my mental energy unnecessarily in the lead-up to games and also a few ways that I have seen other cricketers burn through it unknowingly, only to then be surprised when they had a brain fade due to empty stores of their mental energy.

- Overthinking the upcoming game, or overthinking at any stage during the game.
- Always thinking about match-ups and how I am going to deal with them randomly through the days in the lead-up.
- Allowing myself to have mind chatter about how important this upcoming game is and what happens if I don't perform in this game, including running through all of the potential consequences of getting dropped.

- Online gaming. This was not something I ever did but I have seen many other cricketers gaming for long periods prior to matches.
- Scrolling aimlessly through social media for hours on end. Again, something I didn't do but something that has plagued a lot of players I have played with and against.

I have explained some of the methods I used to deal with my own issues of overthinking and mind chatter in the lead-up to matches. But I do want to address the more modern issues of online gaming and social media.

Professional cricketers were heavily involved in gaming during my playing days. As professional cricketers we do have plenty of down time after training sessions and in the lead-up to matches. A lot of cricketers have moved to gaming as a way to kill time around their training sessions and matches. Since I deeply understood the power of the mind and how important it is to have as much mental energy at your disposal to be the best cricketer you can be, the overstimulation of the brain due to gaming is, for me, totally counterintuitive. Why would people do things that burn through their mental energy stores, like gaming does? There is strong research around gaming and the effect that it has on overstimulating the brain and the recovery time that is needed from this overstimulation. Everything in moderation is fine but when some cricketers are staying up until the early hours of the morning gaming in the lead-up to a cricket match, this needs to be monitored when we are all wanting to bring the best A game that we can.

One common situation that I saw during my latter playing days and into my first season of coaching was players saying after a match that while they were batting they felt really scattered, and couldn't redirect their mind back to one simple thought at a time to get back on track, and it never ended well for them. My first question to them was always about their mental energy stores in the lead-up to the game. They regularly revealed that they had been gaming for a significant part of the day before and into the night in the lead-up to the match. This was a big part of what had caused them to feel scattered while batting.

We need to find other ways to make the time go by in the lead-up to our matches that doesn't excessively burn our mental energy. Even before I understood this about gaming, I always stayed away from it as I had other hobbies. I taught myself how to play the guitar as a 24-year-old, which I found challenging but so unbelievably relaxing and so much fun when I started to jam on tour with my good mate Brett Lee. I also read a lot of books to kill time. At first they were all autobiographies, to learn from other people's experiences in life, and then I moved onto books where I could increase my knowledge around various different topics. Business books have become an obsession in recent times.

Reading and music are known as mindful pastimes. There are many things that you can do which all bring you back to being present and engaged in the moment that don't overstimulate your brain to burn through a lot of your mental energy unnecessarily, such as:

- watching a really good movie that you are fully engaged in
- watching a great TV series that you love and are fully engaged in
- having a proper conversation with a family member or friends where you are deeply listening and engaged in the conversation
- reading a great book
- learning a new hobby, such as a musical instrument or golf
- listening to music — actually listening to the words
- having a 30–60-minute power sleep
- meditation.

One of the best players I have been around over recent times has had some challenges with finding ways to not be 'on' all of the time. This guy is so highly skilled and highly motivated to be the best cricketer he possibly can be, that everything he does and thinks revolves around this goal. In games, he always has a lot on his plate as he is a genuine all-rounder, which means that he needs as much physical and mental energy stores as possible to bring the best version of himself to every game. But in the lead-up to the games he has really struggled to switch off. He struggles to find ways to not overthink things and not be overstimulated. Even watching a movie all the way through, pushing through the slower bits can be a challenge for him. This guy's biggest challenge is to use the various techniques that have been mentioned above to not overstimulate his brain or burn through his mental energy stores unnecessarily so that there is no chance of having any moments of brain fatigue, which can impact his ability to perform consistently at his best. This problem was glaringly obvious to me over the last few years and the individuals and teams who master this skill the best over the next few years will be the most consistently performing teams in the world.

New-age distractions – social media

When I first started my professional cricket career in the early 2000s, social media didn't exist. For me personally, I was a late adopter to social media when it did come into vogue. Around 2009, a few guys in the Aussie team started to get into finding ways to use social media for their benefit. But I was very reluctant to get involved as I was quite regularly the whipping boy for the Aussie media with my inconsistent performances and injury history, so I didn't need to be reading any more opinions saying some not so good things about me.

As time went on, around 2015, I started to get more comfortable with using social media and the opportunities that it could create when used well. You can connect with people who enjoy what you do in different ways. You can also show the true version of you, not just the perceived version of you portrayed by the general media. Commercially it can be fairly lucrative at times as well.

But there is one issue that I see nowadays which is a massive concern when it comes to bringing the best version of you to every performance. A lot of this current generation of players are reading all of the comments that are made about them on social media. There are always a lot of very kind comments, but there's always a few comments from faceless trolls that can hit you really hard. And that little birdie on your shoulder starts talking and gets louder and louder as a result. As human beings, we could get 1000 really kind comments, but then just one not-so-nice comment can get us thinking negatively over and over again and you pick up the shovel and start digging that hole really deep.

So here are the techniques that I used to reduce the emotional toll that social media can take, which in turn can have a significant impact on you bringing the best version of yourself to every performance.

First of all, you can use social media to get things out in the world that you want portrayed, but avoid reading the comments. Have the self-control to not click on the notifications or the comments. Yes, there most probably will be some positive comments, but there is a great chance that there will be one or two negative comments too and these negative comments start to infiltrate your mindset in a big way.

Yes, it is really nice to read nice things and comments about you to build you up, but there is always a downside to it too. By not reading social media about yourself, you don't let the reality of exactly where you are at be infiltrated or warped in any way. If you are following all of the mental skills in this book and are bringing your best possible A factors to every performance and working really hard on continuing to reduce the negative B's in your game, then you don't need an outside perspective, especially not from all of these people who have no idea about exactly where you are at in your mind. If you are honestly critiquing every performance and doing all that you can to bring the best version of you to every performance, this is all that matters and all you can do. You don't want random comments that could be planted into your unconscious mind, where the crew says, 'Aye, aye captain, I will take you there – you do suck!'

An example of this situation came during my last year of playing with CSK in the 2020 IPL in the United Arab Emirates. I was having a conversation with one of our world-class overseas players and giving him my thoughts on how to use social media for the betterment of yourself. I was telling him about not reading any of the comments, and just using the upside of social media to get you out to the world and not letting any of the potential negative comments infiltrate your state of mind. This guy said that he read all of the comments, as the negative ones actually motivated him and provided that fire in the belly to prove those doubters wrong during the games. I said, this is fine for times when you are confident and content with where you are at, but at some stage you are going to have a vulnerable moment, as all of us human beings have, and one comment could really cut you deep and put that shovel in your hand and before you know it you can be 10 feet under, flailing away. And once you are in that deep hole, it can be very hard to get back out.

We played a game the next evening and then had a few days off after that game. I bumped into this guy in the lift on the way to training in the lead-up to our next game and he said, 'That conversation we had, you were right. My last game wasn't my best, and I started to read the comments and a few in particular really hit me hard. I was pretty vulnerable after my not-so-good performance anyway and, before I knew it, I got to a very dark place and found it really hard to get myself out of the hole that was very, very deep.' So from that time on, he never read the comments or clicked on the notifications tab, as he didn't want any outside influences to infiltrate his current state of mind. Without that distraction he could stay in control of his conscious and unconscious mind to bring his best A game to every performance.

KEY TAKEAWAYS

- We only have a certain amount of mental energy every day.

- As diligent as we are with our physical energy stores leading into a game, we need to be as diligent with our mental energy stores as well.

- You need to find the technique that works best for you to get your brain on neutral during down times to conserve as much mental energy as possible and to tap into the power of the gut feel decision-making process.

- Find ways to be totally present in the lead-up to games so that you haven't unnecessarily depleted your mental energy stores.

- Gaming overstimulates your brain, so be very careful when you do engage in gaming in the lead-up to matches.

- Don't look at the comments on your social media channels. Use the power of social media to get the authentic version of you across to the world without exposing yourself to the downside of the trolls that can and will affect your confidence levels.

12

The Holy Grail of Performance

Can I be mentally tough too, or is it just for the chosen few?

What is the true holy grail of performance? For me it is what people term *mental toughness*. I remember growing up watching Steve Waugh, and people saying, 'He's so mentally tough. How good is he? He's as tough as nails.' But what does mental toughness mean? That he is physically tougher than other people? That he could walk through fire as he was so mentally tough? Was he born with this? Was it just how he was, or was it something he learnt? The other players that I played with that really stand out to me being super mentally tough were Ricky

Ponting, Matt Hayden, Glenn McGrath and Shane Warne. No matter the chaos going on around them, they knew how to be at their best and step up when the team needed them to. I wanted to be mentally tough too. But I didn't know exactly what it meant, which meant I didn't know whether I was able to be mentally tough or could develop it.

What mental toughness means in really simple yet powerful terms, is having the ability to singularly focus on the task at hand and just do it over and over again. When there is absolute chaos around you, white noise everywhere, all you do is create a cocoon around yourself and allow that chaos to bounce off. You're totally present and focused on what you need to do at that moment in time. You're focused on the A factors and the process, just bringing the best version of you, ball after ball. Nothing penetrates your bubble. That's what mental toughness is.

It's not being able to run through a brick wall or being physically tough. It's just an ability to control your mind so that nothing distracts it. The wrong things don't penetrate it, only the right things are being put in at the right time for you to access all of your skills.

When I understood that I thought, 'Gosh, I can do that.' Yes, it will take some work to control my internal dialogue, that mind chatter, and understanding that there are B factors that I can't control. But if I keep redirecting the script to be totally present and focused on my best process right now, and let everything else bounce off me, then I thought, 'Wow I can definitely do that.' No one had really explained that to me before so simply and in such a way that I could start to implement it straight away.

Why can't everyone develop mental toughness then? Well, once we know how to do it, then with some practice, we definitely can.

13

Anxiety Affects Performance

How can I eliminate anxiety from impacting my ability to perform?

Anxiety has a look and a feel to it. Some of you may know what it feels like, some of you may know what it looks like. It's that look of worry or dread. You know that look when you see someone with that super blank expression on their face and you think, 'Uh oh, this person is absolutely nowhere.' Or where you look at yourself in the mirror and you think, 'OK, I am really freaking out here.'

It's worrying about what's happened in the past, or what might happen in the future. It's a worry about consequences.

It's worrying about results. Someone who is anxious has moved away from being focused on the task at hand, to focusing on what has happened, or what might happen, the B factors or the result.

FOCUS ON THE TASK AT HAND → WORRY ABOUT FAILURE AND ITS CONSEQUENCES

This concept got reinforced while I was captain of the Sydney Thunder in the BBL. I had a bowler who in the past had bowled great yorkers in the death overs. He also had an awesome change of pace, a great off-cutting slower ball that dipped and bounced. He was starting to push for higher honours and during that period of time he was excellent under pressure for our team. But then out of nowhere, he started to panic a little bit in the death overs. There was one particular game where it had rained heavily and he had to bowl with a wet ball and his front foot was slipping. All of the B factors were against him. But he was struggling in a particular over and when I walked up to him I saw a look of anxiety written all over his face. I thought, 'Uh oh, he's in trouble. He has no chance to execute his skills here and he's going to get launched.' At the time, I didn't understand the concept of anxiety, and worrying about results, taking away someone's ability to focus. I went into the old school cricket captain mode. I said, 'OK mate, this is your field, these are your ball options, and good luck.' Sure enough, he got launched.

I remember walking off the ground and saying to the coach, 'This is the third or fourth time this has happened when we need him. I can't trust him at the back end of the game. I can't bowl him. He just panics.'

That is the conversation that has happened in every cricket team over the ages. You hear captains and coaches talk all the time about trusting players under pressure and when they lose that trust. Instead of helping the player regain it, the reaction is, 'I can't trust him, I'm going to have to find someone else to do it.' So, we dropped him. It was standard practice in almost every cricket team I had ever played in up to that point.

But when I understood how anxiety was affecting his ability to execute his skills and I knew how to redirect his internal script, I realised that I could redirect his focus to what he needed to do right at that moment in time. I could change that anxious look on his face and his ability to execute his skill under pressure too. So, I tested it.

At training, I stood at the top of his mark and talked to him about his technique. I asked him, 'What are your best balls that you bowl under pressure in the death overs? And with that, what are your technical cues to bowl those balls? What are they at the start of your run-up, through your run-up, into your delivery stride, release point and follow through? What is your technical checklist to bowl that particular ball?' I wanted to know so that I could say, 'OK this is the ball you need to bowl, and these are your technical cues that you only need to focus on to execute that ball to the best of your ability.' We worked through this at training to the point where I deeply understood the technical cues he needed to bowl all of his best ball options, which was his wide yorker, his off-cutter slower ball and his fast, hard length.

Then in the game, I tested the theory. First of all, I did not want to allow him to think, or worry, or stress. I was going to tell him which ball he needed to bowl every ball during his over. When I wanted him to bowl a wide yorker, I ran through his technical cues for a wide yorker with him and told him to think about only those things to give himself the best chance of perfect execution. Bang. It worked. He nailed his wide yorker. I did the same for his slower ball. He nailed that as well. His anxiety wasn't there at all! You could see that look on his face change to, 'Yep, I've got this,' instead of, 'Oh no, I am going to get launched.' He was starting to execute his skills under pressure again. He still didn't execute every ball absolutely perfectly, because none of us can do that. We are human beings. But he had a process to return to, to keep him totally present and focused on execution only. We could redirect the script so he was in control and confident, instead of having that look of dread and fear that was previously written all over his face.

That was a real live test for me, and it worked just as the theory said it would. It should be a lesson for coaches and captains. So many are quick to discard players who get that look of fear under pressure and choke and are not able to access their incredible skills because they have allowed their mental environment to be totally corrupted.

But the ability to redirect someone's focus and give them a mental process to eliminate that fear and anxiety could easily turn them around and help them execute the skills that got them into the team in the first place.

Imagine if we all knew this information, including our teammates, our captains and coaches. We would never discard someone who has unbelievable skills at training but can't produce it under pressure in games. We would work with these players to get the best out of them, and have a wider talent pool to choose from and to work with, rather than casting players aside who supposedly aren't up to it because of 'performance anxiety'.

> ## KEY TAKEAWAYS
>
> - Mental toughness is defined as the ability to stay present or task-focused even when there is chaos going on all around you.
> - Mental toughness is available to everyone if you want to develop the skill.
> - Anxiety arises when our mind moves back to what has happened or forward to what might happen in the future.
> - To eliminate anxiety, we need to redirect our thoughts to what we need to do right now to execute our skills to the best of our ability.
> - You can do this for yourself when you see or feel your anxiety starting to build, and you can redirect one of your teammates with the same techniques to help them make their anxiety vanish.

Using the feeling of failure to drive you

One of the worst feelings in the world is that feeling after you have had a shocking performance, where you feel like you have let yourself down and your teammates down. It's that hollow feeling deep inside where you just feel like crap. You find it hard to get to sleep the night after a bad performance because you just keep replaying the situation over and over in your mind. Then you wake up next morning still feeling hollow and you say to yourself, 'I hate this feeling and I don't want to feel like this again.'

For me, this was one of the huge driving forces behind me putting in whatever work that I needed to in the lead-up to the next game, to give myself the best chance of having a better game, so I didn't feel like that again. This shocking feeling can drive you to sacrifice whatever you need to in order to give yourself the best chance of having a much better game next time.

After I was equipped with better mental skills, I used this feeling as a driver for me to do whatever I could to be in control of bringing my very best A game. Every single moment in the lead-up to the game and especially during the game, I did everything I could to give myself the best chance of being at my best.

The question that I ask all the people I now work with is: Now that you know that you are in control of the A part of the performance equation, are you desperate enough, committed enough, disciplined enough, to exercise this control with single-minded discipline to bring the best version of you and significantly reduce the chances of reproducing that horrible feeling that we all get after one of those bad days?

14

The Rules of the Mental Road

The rules of the mental road are a play on the rules of the road. There are seven rules of the mental road to govern our thinking, to bring the best version of ourselves every time we need to perform. Each rule has two sides to them, the 'self-sabotaging your performance' side, and the 'getting out of your own way' side. And there were two rules in particular that instantly made me realise that I could get back to my best.

Rule #1

If you want to climb out of a hole, the very first thing you must do is stop digging.

This is all about the internal dialogue we have in our minds. The little birdie on our shoulder. The negative thoughts that dig us into a massive hole in the first place. I was a master at digging! I used to have a big shovel and was flailing away at a rapid rate. 'How come I got out? I'm as weak as piss. I needed to score runs today. I'm mentally weak. Have I lost it? I've let myself down. I am the reason why we lost. Am I going to lose my spot in the team?'

The first thing you must do is to listen to your mind chatter and realise you are digging, and then put the shovel down. Most of us allow our minds to move that way. We allow the script to move in that direction. Most of us don't realise that we have a shovel in our hand and we're flailing away digging the hole, and we have the ability to put the shovel down. This refers to one of the key functions of the conscious mind. You are in control of your conscious mind and you need to exercise that control that you have over your mind chatter.

Prior to 2015, whenever I got out, my default was to start digging furiously. Especially in a big game. I would say all sorts of negative things to myself. After I became aware of this rule, I was able to understand that I was in control of this script. When those thoughts crept in, I listened in and was able to say, 'Stop it! This is counterproductive. This is not where I need to go at all.' If you let these thoughts roll, before you know it you're digging pretty deep and beating yourself up. And the deeper the hole, the harder it is to get out of. My strategy, once I identified I was digging, was to ask myself, 'OK, what happened? Why did it happen? Was the outcome influenced by something that was outside of my control? How can I do it better so there's less chance of it happening next time? Is it something I can work on at training or is it simply a case of making sure in the next game I do it differently so there's less chance of it happening again?' Once I had asked those questions and answered them, I instantly moved forward in a much more productive way.

KEY TAKEAWAYS

- Listen into your mind chatter and as soon as you hear yourself starting to dig, you need to immediately put down the shovel.
- The deeper the hole gets, the harder it is to climb out, so always listen in so that you can climb out of the hole while it is still pretty shallow.

Rule #2

The conscious mind can only actively process one thought at a time.

This concept was the most powerful for me, in terms of turning my anxiety and fear around. The person who first mentioned this to me was Justin Langer in 2005. Justin gave me the what, just as Michael Clarke and Glenn McGrath did with the putting a song in their head. 'Just put the right thing in your mind,' Justin said. 'The most important thing is the ball. So just put that in your mind, watch the ball, because that's the most important thing.' But it was never explained why. And not knowing the why, I found it much harder to embed it into my ball-by-ball routine. Because if I knew why, then I would have continued to do it over and over again, realising the power of it. And knowing the why meant that I would know how important it was to go back to it when I started to go off-track. I needed to understand the science behind it in terms of how the conscious mind functions. If the right thing goes into your mind, at the right time, then the wrong thing can't come in. If your conscious mind has the right thought, your unconscious mind will act on it because you are then tapping into the unconscious mind where all of your deeply ingrained skills and instincts sit.

It was this rule that I broke time and again in the last period of my Test career in 2015, after the tragic event where my good mate had passed away after being hit. A huge amount of anxiety around facing the short ball had all of a sudden come into my game. Every time I knew someone had a good short ball, even if they only bowled at 130 kph but had a good bouncer, that was the thing that flew into my mind as the ball was delivered. I was allowing mental space, keeping my mind clear to just watch the ball, and then bang, 'short ball' popped into my mind, even if it wasn't a short ball.

A good example of this was the last Test match that I ever played. It was in Cardiff, Wales, in the first Test of the 2015 Ashes series. This was right in the midst of my struggles prior to getting educated on this information. In both innings I was out lbw. I got out in the first innings to Stuart Broad, and in the second innings I fell to Mark Wood. But in both innings right as the ball was bowled, the thought of 'short ball' flew into my mind. I thought it was going to be a short ball because I allowed the little voice to say the wrong thing rather than controlling the little voice. As a result, I was out of position thinking that it was going to be a short ball and then got out lbw. Everyone took the piss out of me because I was out lbw again. I never revealed it at the time because I was still trying to hang on to my Test career.

Facing fast bowling was always one of my biggest strengths as a batter.

I was totally fearless. Yes, I knew if I got unlucky, I could get hurt pretty badly, like breaking an arm or getting hit on a bad spot around my head and get concussed; never did I think that I could get hit and be instantly killed. After the tragic event I witnessed, fear came into my batting while facing fast bowling. I was thinking that this could happen to me as well. And I wasn't equipped with the mental skills, and rule number 2 in particular, to understand how to override this fear that was having such an impact on my ability to perform. I was corrupting my own performances by the fear of the short ball and the impact that it could have on my life. If I had told my coach at that time what was actually going on in my head, then he would have been very kind and understanding. But at the same time he might have said, 'OK, thanks for telling me and I really feel for you, but I need to get someone who is not affected by these kinds of thoughts.'

To play the short ball well, you need to play it totally on instinct. You have to practise it so much to ensure that your instincts get you into the right position to play it really well. If you use your conscious mind to see it and play it, you will be way too slow on it. What I was doing wrong was, I was consciously thinking it was going to be a short ball so if it was a short ball, I was consciously trying to play it. I was always slow on the shot. And then if it wasn't a short ball, I was totally out of position as well so I was exposed to other ways of getting out.

Once I deeply understood this rule, my life changed. If I put the right thought into my mind, then the wrong thought couldn't come in. For me, I was allowing space in my mind as the ball was about to be bowled, which was allowing the wrong thought to fly in. So, if this was true, all I needed to do to sort this out was to put the right thought in my mind at the right time so that the wrong thing, short ball, couldn't come in.

Even if I still got a bit anxious, and I did, knowing someone is bowling fast and has a good short ball, I knew how to override it so it wouldn't affect my performance. I knew I might not be feeling that comfortable. But I knew how to still perform at my best by putting the right thought in my conscious mind at the right time and letting my ingrained instincts take over.

I put this to the test in the latter stages of my career in the Pakistan Super League and the IPL in particular. I remember facing Pakistan left-arm quick Mohammad Irfan, who is about seven-foot tall and could bowl at really good pace with extra bounce that he could extract off any pitch. Straight away I was thinking, 'Uh oh, he's got a good short ball.' I was fighting myself. That little birdie on my shoulder started to say, 'He could do some damage to you here.' But knowing now how to override this, all I did was jam the word 'aggressive' into my mind at the right time. And the timing of this was also important. Not before, or after, but right on the release of the ball, so the wrong thing couldn't come in at the wrong time. Then I knew that I was letting my instincts take over and I wasn't premeditating the short ball. I was just in a good position to play whatever delivery came my way.

And it was like that every time I faced someone who I knew had good pace from that time on. I faced a lot of guys like Wahab Riaz and Jasprit Bumrah and played them well, as I did when I was younger, and I didn't have the fear going through my mind, as I knew how to overwrite that fear with the right thought at the right time so my performance was never affected again.

Counting backwards from 100

Here is a very simple exercise to reinforce that your mind can only actively process one thought at a time. I want you to count backwards from 100 in threes. But at some point get someone to throw in a random simple mathematical equation. So start, '100, 97, 94', and then at 91 get the person to say '2 × 3?' and then keep counting backwards until 82. OK, now stop. So what has happened here is you started counting back in threes, then once the simple mathematical equation was given, you stopped counting and gave the answer, '6'. Then straight away, you had to remember where you left off counting and continued on. '88, 85, 82.' Not everyone is amazing at maths but even if you were and could do the equation quickly, you would still have to stop counting and say 6 before resuming counting down. You couldn't say 6 and 91 at the same time. It just reinforces that your mind can only actively process one thought at a time.

Multi-tasking

People always say, 'I'm great at multi-tasking.' But what actually is multi-tasking? It's essentially task switching, doing one thing and then moving onto the next thing without completing the first thing, and then moving back and forth between these things, or several others, very quickly. Although people may think they are doing tasks at the same time, they are really not. You can go from task one, to task three, back to task two. You're on your computer, you receive a message, something else arises, you check your phone, then you go back to task one and finish that, then you move on to task five. Multi-tasking is just jumping from task to task.

Sometimes we're in a situation where we need to juggle several tasks within a small window of time. We need to understand that the most effective way to finish these tasks relies on controlling our focus to be on one thing at a time. We need to prioritise the things that we need to do, then shift our focus to a single task and focus fully on that task. Then, when the situation warrants it, shift our focus to the second task and fully focus on that task. If we don't focus on one task at a time, we end up switching between tasks, instead of remaining fully focused on a single task, one at a time. For example, chefs can have so many moving parts that they need to bring together just for one specific dish. And for them to do it most effectively, they need to pay attention to what they're doing right at that moment for each separate component of that dish and do it over and over again until the dish is ready to serve. So the key is to control the task switching while being fully focused on the thing that we're doing at that time. This is the simple definition of multi-tasking.

But in a perfect world, if you want to do something efficiently, with the least amount of drain on your mental energy, you need to focus on one task and just get it off your plate. If you do want to get through a task well, then you need to limit distractions and shut the external noise out. When we want to get something done as efficiently as possible, we need to turn off any distraction. That might be your phone, the notifications on your computer, you might need to lock your room, whatever you need to do to not allow yourself to be distracted at all, which in this day and age, is incredibly difficult to do.

What is the secret to shutting out the distractions? People will say, 'You need to focus more! You need to focus harder!'

But the secret isn't to focus more or harder. The secret is to focus correctly.

The art of focus – how do I maintain my focus without burning myself out?

Once you are focused correctly, then you can focus more and focus harder. This was the mistake I made in my career. I was burning mental energy like it was going out of fashion at the non-striker's end, when I should have been totally tuned out with my mind on neutral. I was focused, but I was focused on the wrong thing at the wrong time.

If you are incorrectly focused and then you focus more, then you are shooting yourself in the foot with a bigger gun. The key is not to focus more – it is to focus correctly.

Ricky Ponting gave me the clearest example of how he did this. He used rule number 2 throughout his whole career. We talked about batting so much but it was almost always around the technical side of batting. I never asked him about his mental skills techniques until I interviewed him on my podcast. If I knew why he did this during my career, it would have helped me so much in terms of not allowing any noise to penetrate my bubble. He said the following during the interview:

When the bowler was at the top of his mark, I just said 'watch the ball' once when he started his run up. When he was halfway in I said it again. And when he jumped into his delivery stride, I said 'watch the ball' again. That's not about me telling myself I had to watch the ball because I wasn't good at watching the ball. But it was about keeping all the other thoughts out. If I said one thing, I didn't allow anything else to get into my head. I didn't allow that premeditation of 'a short ball is coming, I'm going to pull it if it's short,' or 'this is going to be a full one, I'm going to drive it down the ground if it's full'. I battled those things early in my career. As a young bloke looking to impress and looking to dominate, I had those thoughts in my head. I then worked it out and kept things a bit simpler. I knew if I could keep giving myself one thought, and that was always just to watch the ball, that was to keep my head clear. Then all the practice and everything that I did could then take over. I've been playing this game since I was six or seven, eight years of age. It wasn't like any of that was going to go anywhere. But if I had a clouded mind, then I wasn't letting my body do the things that I've tried to do for so long. So that was the basis of my batting when I got out to the middle.

He was never instructed to do this by anyone trying to educate him on mental skills, but this explanation is the exact embodiment of rule number 2.

I saw Ricky tell himself to watch the ball constantly. I saw him do it from 22 yards away. But I never asked why. I wish I had known why he did it. He was correctly focused, so he couldn't be incorrectly focused.

KEY TAKEAWAYS

- Your mind can only process one thought at one moment in time.

- Put the right thought in your mind so the wrong thought can't come in.

- The key is to focus correctly, not focus more.

- Multi-tasking is switching from one task to the next and back again. It is not doing two things at the same time.

Rule #3

You can't not think about whatever is on your mind.

I want you to do another simple exercise for me. I don't want you to think about the next thing I'm going to describe to you. I don't want you to picture in your mind's eye a huge … pink … elephant … with blue and yellow polka-dot shorts. It's hard to do, isn't it? How would you not picture this pink elephant? You would have to focus on something else, like a blue lion with a yellow tail. You would need to focus intently and correctly on this blue lion to remove the image of the pink elephant with blue and yellow polka-dot shorts from your mind.

It's a simple concept, but rule number 3 just reinforces rule number 2. If you are trying to not think about failing or making a mistake, guess what you're going to think about? Failing or making that mistake.

Ricky gave another example of this concept on my podcast talking about his coaching philosophy in the IPL:

I'm so conscious of what I say to guys now as a result of understanding the power of the mind. If I was a captain or a coach and I tell a bowler 'don't bowl a wide, don't bowl a wide' and you leave them with that thought, well what do they do? Because you leave them with 'don't bowl a wide', they bowl a wide because that's the last thing they're thinking about, right? But if you tell them to 'run in and bowl the perfect ball' or 'run in and bowl a perfect yorker', give them that positive thought and that positive image, then they will more than likely do that for you.

This was the same thing I did with the bowler from Sydney Thunder. I put the technical cues in his mind as he was running in so he couldn't worry about the outcome. It's so simple. The only way not to think about the pink elephant is to put something else in your mind. That's the power of rule number 3 and the power of understanding how to create the right mental environment to be able to access your skills. Put the right thing in your mind so the wrong thing can't come in, and if the wrong thing starts to come in, just redirect it with the right thing and you will be totally fine.

KEY TAKEAWAYS

- As soon as you are starting to think about not making a mistake, guess what you are exactly thinking about?
- Once you identify that you are trying not to think about failing, then redirect your thought to the right thing, by using the power of rule number 2.

Rule #4

Your dominant thought controls your ability to perform, including your emotions.

PENDULUM CROSS

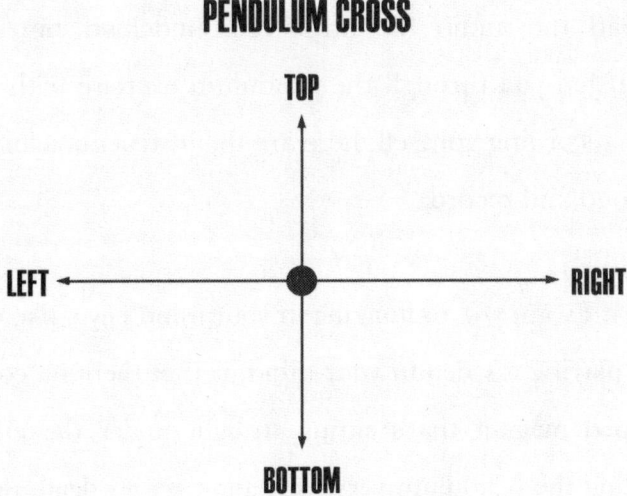

147

There is an exercise I want you to do to deeply understand this rule. It involves a pendulum and the cross that has four arrows, left and right, top and bottom. People have successfully used a phone charger cord with an earphones case attached to it. The other option is to take a light string or thin chain (about 30 cm long) and tie a washer, heavy paperclip or fishing weight to one end to make a pendulum. I want you to hold the end of the pendulum in your dominant hand. It is my left hand for me as I write left-handed even though I threw and bowled right-handed. Hold it with just your thumb and forefinger and your elbow resting on the table. Hover the pendulum one centimetre above the centre of the cross and I want you to keep your eyes open and hand still. Now that you know the starting position for this exercise, I need you to get your phone out and record in voice notes these instructions that are below. Or you can download the audio file http://on.soundcloud.com/XpafC where I step you through the pendulum exercise with you. If you are recording yourself, here are the instructions for you to read aloud and record:

What I want you to imagine in your mind's eye, like you are playing a video in your mind, is that there's a cone-shaped magnet that's sitting straight under the circle pulling the pendulum very, very tight, so it's dead, dead still. This magnet is so strong that it's pulling the pendulum dead tight and dead still. Now I am taking the magnet away. And I want you to imagine the pendulum starts moving from left to right, it slowly starts moving from left to right. Imagine in your mind's eye, the pendulum just starting to swing from left to right, very slowly, moving left to right. And it gradually gets bigger and bigger. Swinging out wider and wider. Keep imagining in your mind's eye it going from left to right. And going as wide as you can swing out as far to the sides as it possibly can, left to right, left to right, keep imagining it going left to right. Now I want you to imagine that the cone-shaped magnet comes back straight underneath the circle and pulls the pendulum dead tight and dead still. Just imagine that really strong magnet, just coming underneath and just pulling the pendulum dead still and hovering dead still straight over the middle of the circle. Now the strong magnet moves out from underneath again. I want you to imagine the pendulum moving in a clockwise direction around the circle, starting to move slowly around in a clockwise direction, around the cross, going right around and gradually going wider and wider and going out to the sides and up to the top and just swinging around and around and around and getting wider and bigger and wider and trying to touch the sides. Keep imagining it touching the sides of the arrows going around and around and around. And now I want you to imagine the magnet coming straight back onto the middle of the circle and pulling it dead still, dead tight again. The pendulum has a really strong magnet just holding it really, really tight. Until it's dead still.

Before you get started, I want you to understand a couple of key points. I want you to just listen to the instructions that you have recorded without deliberately moving the pendulum. You need to imagine in your mind's eye all of the instructions. The aim of this exercise isn't to keep the pendulum still but I don't want you to deliberately move it. If the pendulum moves while using your imagination correctly, then allow it to move. If the pendulum stays still, that is fine as well. Follow these instructions carefully and imagine them in your mind's eye as you hold the pendulum above the cross.

When I did this exercise for the first time, to my amazement, the pendulum moved in the exact way described, without my fingers or arm physically moving it.

Let me explain what had happened from a scientific standpoint. Imagine there are sensors on all of the muscles around your arm to see what the firing patterns of the muscles are. If I had told you to deliberately move the pendulum from side to side left to right and clockwise around the circle, your muscles would fire in a certain pattern to move the pendulum. But when you imagine it, or visualise in your mind's eye the pendulum moving, your muscles fire in exactly the same manner but because you are imagining it, in electrical terms it's like the dimmer switch on a light being turned right down to a low setting. But the switch is still on, so you can see the pendulum moving.

What this exercise taught me, in conjunction with rule number 5, was how unbelievably powerful your unconscious mind is. If you visualise something in your conscious mind, the crew, the unconscious mind, says, 'We've got it, we will take you there.' Yes, it's with the dimmer switch or the volume turned down, but the crew will still act on it. And this is the power of visualisation and imagery.

If you say to yourself, 'I'm not hitting the ball very well today' or 'This bowler gives me trouble' or 'Don't get out', guess which direction the pendulum is going to move? It's starting to move that way. It doesn't mean that you definitely will get out, but you're starting to move the pendulum in that direction. So you need to be super vigilant over what you think about, and what you're actually putting into the conscious mind, which then filters down so powerfully to your unconscious mind.

After I did this pendulum exercise and deeply understood the power of the unconscious mind, from that moment on, I was so careful with what my internal dialogue was. By understanding the most important conscious mind function – that we are in control of our thoughts – then in conjunction, understanding how powerful the unconscious mind is in acting on those thoughts by seeing it first hand through the powerful pendulum exercise, I knew I had to take control. I wanted to be the best I could be every time I went out to play. I wanted to score runs and take wickets every time I went out to play. To give myself the best chance of this happening, I had to control my mind to direct the pendulum in the right way. So as soon as I heard thoughts like, 'What happens if I get out now', or 'Now is not a good time to get out', or 'What happens if I get this ball wrong?', straight away I would catch those thoughts and redirect them to the right thoughts. The right thoughts for me were all about the technical execution of that ball, and having an aggressive mindset with no fear. I consistently redirected my thoughts. Yes, some days it was harder to redirect my mind than others. But these were the days where I brought the best version of myself, which were more often than not the days where I got the better results.

There are times when I've run this exercise where the pendulum doesn't move. Sometimes that happens because the instructions have not been clear enough or the person doing the exercise misinterprets that they must keep the pendulum dead still throughout. In which case, the pendulum will stay still. Sometimes, very rarely, the person doing the exercise is determined to prove the exercise wrong by saying to themselves, 'I am not going to let this guy get into my head!' And they willingly disobey the instructions, which also means that the pendulum doesn't move.

But the majority of the time, if you allow the instructions into your thoughts and vividly imagine what is being described, then it will move every single time because you are just tapping into your unconscious mind. That's the power of this entire ACT Model that we will define for you in the next few chapters. Through your conscious mind, you are pushing the right thought into your unconscious mind and the crew takes you there. It's moving the pendulum in the right direction to get the best out of what you've got in that moment in time. The pendulum exercise is a really simple hypnosis technique where you are allowing someone to dictate what you are visualising by directing your thoughts. That's what hypnosis is. It is guided imagery. The key is learning how to dictate your own thoughts.

Before I go any further, I need to define the important differences between visualisation and imagery. Visualisation is defined mainly around what you see in your mind's eye without including our other senses. Whereas imagery defines what we see in our mind's eye as well as incorporating all of our senses (including vision) into our imagery practice. It allows us to imagine the situation using all of our senses and the more we use all of our senses, the more powerful the mental rehearsal is. The two approaches to imagery are the 'do mode' and a 'view mode'. In 'do mode' you see the action (and remember what it feels like when you do it that way) as though you were looking through your own eyes. In 'view mode' you see yourself executing the task as though you were watching yourself on video. 'Do mode' is generally more powerful because not only do you see the action of your performance through your own eyes, but it is often easier to incorporate what the action 'feels like' when you do it the right way. You incorporate more of your senses in 'do mode' imagery, as opposed to only considering what you see in your mind's eye (only using your visual channel).

Knowing that if I imagine the pendulum moving and it does, with the volume turned down, this reinforces how powerful visualisation can be as a skills development tool. If I can deeply imagine my body moving in a certain way, reacting to a certain ball that is bowled to me, or executing technically a certain delivery that I want to bowl, then these neural pathways start to be developed and build, without even having to go to training to do this physically. Yes, the volume is turned down, so these neural pathways, the muscle memory won't be as strong, but it is a powerful tool to use even when you don't have an opportunity to get out into the middle. We need to understand that this does take quite a bit of mental energy to use this very powerful technique, so in the lead-up to a game we want to use it at the right time so that when we go out into the middle we have as much mental energy as possible. But done at the right time and done correctly, visualisation or imagery can be very powerful skills to develop and reinforce great execution of our skills, to develop our skills by tapping into the power of the unconscious mind.

Imagery – watching video footage of you performing at your best

Your body can't tell the difference between what is real or what is vividly imagined in your mind, so we can use all of this power in different ways. Matt Hayden used imagery before each Test match. He would sit on the pitch for up to 45 minutes the day before the game, mentally rehearsing all of his skills, who would be bowling to him, what balls they would bowl, and he would see himself reacting perfectly to each of these balls. This was Matt Hayden in 'do mode', which is visualising yourself performing out of your own eyes, seeing exactly what it looks like being in your own body and trying to imagine what it feels like.

Another technique with visualisation is watching video footage of you at your best in 'view mode'. This is you seeing yourself performing your skill from another perspective, from outside your body, which is what you are doing when you watch video footage of yourself performing at your best. Brett Lee used to do this on the team bus on the way to the ground, which caused him to be the brunt of a few sledges from us teammates who were taking the piss out of him a bit while he watched himself celebrating after seeing the stumps flying everywhere. None of us really understood the power of this, but Binga did. Seeing the best version of himself would build up that all important confidence and remind him of the best technical and mental version of himself that he knew he had in him to take it into the game. We just thought Binga was being very self-indulgent. How wrong we were! Everyone else would be watching footage of the opposition, what their strengths and weaknesses were, but none of us were watching footage of us at our best to reinforce that super version of ourselves.

Once I understood the power of this 'view mode' before every game, during the 45 minutes that I would set aside for my preparation time, I would watch footage of myself during my very best innings over the previous few years. I would do this for two reasons. First of all, it was a way to maybe pick up anything technically that was different to how I was batting at that moment in time. Occasionally, I would pick up something, like if I was moving into my forward press too late. When I was at my best, I always made sure my pre-movement was done early so that my head was dead still as the ball was bowled. In T20 cricket, two other technical things would normally stick out. One was that I was using my shoulder coil to swing my bat so I could uncoil right through the line of the ball. When I wasn't using my shoulders to swing my bat, especially when I was power hitting in a T20 game, my bat swing would be much faster than normal and my bottom hand would be taking over, which meant I normally could only access half of the ground, from dead straight around to the leg side. When I was coiling my front shoulder, then I was watching the ball right onto my bat and not coming up out of the shot too early. I was powering the ball through the off side as well as straight and to the leg side.

The other little thing that I would pick up a lot of the time was that I was a little lower in my stance, which meant I had more power in my legs to power up and through the ball. At times I could feel too tall on the ball, as though I was above the ball, which made it much more difficult to power the ball deep into the stands. When I was lower, engaging my legs, I could power up through the ball without thinking about it, which would get the powerful elevation without trying to lean back and hit it up. I was trying to tap into my inner AB de Villiers.

Arguably the most important thing that I would get out of watching my best innings was the reinforcement of my best mindset that was always on display during my best innings. The fearless, aggressive freedom to take down the bowlers, the full aggressive commitment to every ball that I was facing was so obvious when I was at my best. Watching footage of these best days reinforced that fearless, aggressive mindset that I always had when I was dominating world-class bowling attacks in all conditions. Combining this with working through my ACT Model in my diary during that 45 minutes would just get me ready to bring my best A game mindset to the game that I was about to play.

Funnily enough, there was a situation in the 2013 Ashes, prior to deeply understanding this information, where I watched footage of two other players who I admired that helped me tap into that fearless, aggressive mindset. I didn't know the power of it at the time, but I was struggling with getting out lbw in the first three Tests. I was trying to work out why I was getting in trouble in the Test matches when I didn't have the same issues of getting out lbw in limited-overs cricket. Prior to the 4th Test in Durham I watched footage of Viv Richards making 291 for the West Indies against England at the Oval in 1976. I also watched Ian Botham's 1981 masterclass at Headingley against Australia, when he smashed 149 not out to help England produce a miracle comeback. Both had their own minor technical deficiencies as all batters do, but what struck me about watching both of them was the intent they showed. Their presence at the crease and their aggressive and fearless mindset was inspiring. It put me in the right mindset to go and play the way that I wanted to play. As a result of finding that mindset through watching Viv and Beefy, I went out and made 68 in the 4th Test at Durham and then 176 in the 5th Test at the Oval, which was my highest Test score and one of my best innings.

KEY TAKEAWAYS

- We need to be so unbelievably careful with what thoughts we have in our conscious mind as the pendulum will start to move this way, with the unconscious mind taking you there, with the dimmer switch turned down.
- When we put the right images or thoughts into our conscious mind, the power of the unconscious mind takes over and moves the pendulum in this direction.
- Using imagery in 'do mode' is the most powerful

form of mental rehearsal but visualisation or 'view mode' is still very powerful.

- Your body can't tell the difference between reality and what you vividly imagine in your mind's eye, which is an amazing training tool in preparation for a game or developing the muscle memory for a new skill.

Rule #5

You are in control of your dominant thought!

This is a simple reinforcement of rule number four. You are in control of your dominant thought. Your dominant thought is your conscious thought. This rule reinforces that you are in control of your conscious thought and how incredibly important it is to exercise that control, knowing that the pendulum will move in the direction of your dominant thought.

If you make the most of the control that you have over your conscious thought, your unconscious mind, the crew, will always agree and say we've got this, we will take you there. Exercising control of the A factors in the performance equation and controlling your mindset means you will always bring the best version of yourself to every performance. This is the rule that is critical to revisit whenever doubts creep in. You are always in control of your mind. Make the most of the control that you have.

> **KEY TAKEAWAY**
>
> - The most important function of the conscious mind is that we are in control of it, so we need to exercise this power that we have to bring out the best versions of ourselves every time.

Rule #6

Glass half full or glass half empty? Understand the importance of perspective.

This is really all about perspective and understanding how important your perspective is.

When I went over to visit Jacques Dallaire in 2015, I thought he was going to break me down into a blubbering mess, and then rebuild me from the ground up. But in the end, both rule number two − *the conscious mind can only actively process one thought at a time* − and this rule − number six, which Jacques explained to me over a period of 10 to 15 minutes, about how important your perspective is, immediately shifted my mindset to say, 'OK, I can definitely turn all of this around.'

My perspective after Phillip Hughes died was that there's a great chance that the next ball could have the same impact on my life and my family. I had seen it happen right in front of my own eyes. With the next ball, in my mind, there was a chance of that happening to me. I got asked a few simple yet powerful questions to put this incredibly tragic event into some sort of perspective. 'Has anyone been killed before playing cricket, like this?' I thought, no, not that I know of. Jacques said, 'OK, so how many balls had been bowled up until that point? How many balls had been bowled in cricket up until that event happened?' Millions and millions, I thought. Most probably billions if you include professional cricket, club cricket, social cricket, everything. He said, 'So there is a one in a billion/s chance of this happening again?' Well, yeah. 'So, the chances of the next ball having that effect specifically on you is a one in a billion/s chance. That's pretty remote.' I thought, OK, I get that.

Then he asked, 'Have the safety precautions improved since the event?' I said, yes, they have stem guards now on the back of the helmets that actually protect the brainstem area in addition to the normal helmet protecting the skull. He said, 'Are you wearing them?' I said no, I'm not wearing it because I feel really enclosed. I just don't feel comfortable. I've never felt comfortable wearing them. He said, 'So there's a one in a billion chance of the event happening, and you can wear these things that protect that one area of the neck that is exposed, and you're not wearing it, and you've got a fear of that event happening to you, which is having a massive impact on your performances? Just practise with it and get used to it.' That makes sense, I thought.

He then asked, 'Have you really practised against that particular ball? Have you really been practising that shot and that ball?' I said, not really. I knew I needed to but as soon as I got someone to throw balls at me, I started to get super anxious and stopped after about 10 balls. So, no, I hadn't. Jacques then said, 'You need to practise it. You need to relearn that shot, so you can then deeply trust your instincts. So you can trust that you're going to get in a really good position, and not have the fear of being exposed to this happening to you.'

The first thing I did when I went home was get the stem guards and I got used to wearing them immediately. Then I really relearnt how to play the short ball again. It was like I was back at the Cricket Academy as an 18-year-old. I started with tennis balls being underarmed at me and built up from there. In the end, I got to a stage where I was getting my strength and conditioning coach from Cricket New South Wales, the great Paul Chapman, to throw balls at me from half-pitch. They were hard cricket balls and bouncers every single ball. He would then throw a full ball in there randomly to make sure I was reacting instinctively to the ball that was coming down and not just premeditating a short ball.

I got to a stage where I was super confident, trusting my instincts, and I was getting into really good positions. From that moment on, I knew my performance wasn't going to be affected by this ball anymore. I used rule number two, to put the right thing in my mind at the right time. I didn't allow my mind to premeditate a short ball and let myself be out of position. I had been trying to play the short ball with my conscious mind prior to learning these rules. Playing the pull shot, playing the short ball is very reactive. It's totally an unconscious shot, played well with your unconscious mind. It's total instinct.

By retraining my technique to ensure that my instincts were as good as could be, I was able to trust that there was a very minimal chance now of getting into trouble by getting into a bad position. And now, even when I did get a little anxious out in the middle by facing someone who was bowling fast, which always happened as the scars were so deep, I knew how to override those feelings by putting the right thing into my mind at the right time and my performance would never be affected by this again. And it wasn't.

This is the power of perspective and how important the right perspective is. If my wife, Lee, asked me about how I was dealing with my good mate's passing, I would just shut it down. I had no way of coping with this tragic event apart from trying to shut that part of my brain down to try to shut it out. But just learning this perspective rule, and understanding how important your perspective is, put me right back on track immediately. I never felt comfortable opening up to anyone about where I was at with this tragic event, so I had no chance of getting the right perspective on that tragic event. I definitely couldn't have told my coach at the time or any players around me that I was petrified that the next ball from a fast bowler could have the same impact on my life. And I definitely didn't feel I could trust any psychologist around the team too, just in case it got back to the coach and or selectors. The first thing they would have done is say, 'Oh, we really feel for you that this tragic event has had this impact on you.' But I feared in the next breath they would say, 'But we are going to drop you, as we need someone to be playing this Ashes series who isn't affected like this, as we need batters who are at the top of their game, not someone who is in the head space you are.'

I am sure that I wasn't the only batter during that Ashes series who was fighting the exact same demons and whose performances were affected significantly, just like mine.

In the end, if I was asked these questions the day after Phil died, yes, it still would have been incredibly raw, but I would have been able to work through it to put this tragic event into perspective a lot quicker, instead of nine months down the track, having spent those nine months thinking the next ball could have the same effect on my life and my family. What I learned was that you need to be very, very careful about what your perspective is on any given event. Because there are always two sides to the same event – the same glass could be filled up halfway, but depending on how you see it, it can be a glass half full or a glass half empty.

A way to reinforce the importance of perspective is to look at the image below and consider: is your perspective accurate?

IS YOUR PERSPECTIVE ACCURATE?

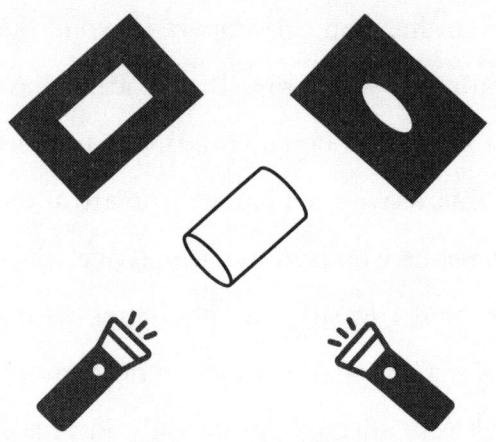

I've got a torch and I'm shining it on the cylinder. If I shine the torch from one side of the cylinder, the shadow projected onto the wall will be a rectangular shape. But if I move the torch 90 degrees to the left and shine the torch from a different angle on the cylinder, the shadow on the wall is a circular shape. Depending on your perspective, and which side of the cylinder you are on, the same object can appear to be two different shapes. How can the same thing appear to be so different? It depends on your perspective and what side you see it from. It just reinforces how careful you need to be on what your perspective is. The same event can have two different perspectives, depending on what your past is, or what you initially feel.

There's a glass half-full perspective or one that sees the glass as half empty. It's your choice. You're in control of which way you take it and your mind moves the pendulum in that direction.

KEY TAKEAWAYS

- Every event in your life is neutral but you have a choice every time on what your perspective of that event is going to be.

- Even with a tragic event occurring, you need to be aware of your perspective and pick the most productive perspective even in horrific situations, as you do have a choice.

- Do you want to be the optimist or the pessimist depending on your perspective? That always has a significant impact on our ability to perform.

Rule #7

If you do what you've always done, you will get what you have always got. If you want something different, then you need to approach the same situation with a different mindset!

There is a well-known definition of insanity: doing the same thing over and over again and expecting a different result. We have the power to change our thoughts and to change our behaviours. We have the power to overwrite our old habits if we approach things from a different perspective and with a different mindset.

You can take your same technical skills and know-how into any pursuit, but if you approach it with a different mindset you will get a different result. Whereas if you take the same set of skills and keep approaching them with the same, often corrupted, mindset, ignoring the rules of the mental road, you will get the same results. That's the power of being able to approach things in a different way. This is simple information to be able to change your approach immediately.

KEY TAKEAWAYS

- Approaching the same events with a different mindset will mean you will get a different result and have a much better chance of being on the right side of the result.

15

ACT Model Development – The Secret Sauce

This is what we've been working towards. I've set the stage for this process by sharing with you a lot of background information that will help you to understand how unbelievably powerful the ACT Model is and how and why it works as it does. This book has given you a deliberate progression of thought to this point so that you could learn all of the necessary information along the way to help execute what we're about to work through.

The ACT Model, with practice, is a superpower for you to tap into every time you need to perform. It is a self-directed conscious-mind rudder-control process to allow you to tap into your unconscious mind. It is a process to unlock your best performance every time. It gives you a clear process to step into your optimal mindset every time and gives you the control to be able to step into that mindset consistently, rather than hoping that the seas part and you fall into your best performance mindset.

Getting rid of your old habits

I didn't realise it, but I had become a product of a lifetime of bad habits from a mental skills perspective. Throughout my cricket career, from age 16 right up until age 34, I had placed enormous pressure on myself to get the results I was desperate for. Most of us have experienced this and developed these types of bad habits. These habits are often influenced and reinforced by feedback from our environment and from important individuals in our life. That happened a lot to me from coaches, players and teams that I was in. This feedback can often be positive and productive. But a lot of the time, as it was in my case, it can also be negative and counterproductive. I was so infatuated with results and based my whole value and success as a human being around being the best cricketer possible, partly because that was the environment I was in.

When it comes time to change our mindset, however, we need to remember that the mind is different from a computer in that we can't simply erase an old habit like we can a file on a flash drive. We must overwrite the old program with a new, more powerful one! Negative thinking can only be changed by relearning different, more effective, and more powerful thought processes. To do so, we must become aware of what we want to change and then consciously repeat the new thought pattern over and over again in our mind to embed the new thinking into our unconscious mind. That's how we create better mental habits and bring out the best version of ourselves more often.

Intensity and performance

How does my intensity level affect my performance?

There's an optimum level of intensity for each of us. When it comes to finding the right sort of intensity levels in your own mind, everyone is slightly different. Some people may need different intensity levels for different scenarios. Some people need to be revving a bit higher. They need to push the limits of where they need to be. Whereas other people just need to get into their own bubble. They just need to be a little bit intense. It's all about finding the right amount for your optimum performance. You've just got to understand where you sit and define exactly where you are on the spectrum. Because you may need to be revving higher as you're not intense enough, which is the edge you need to be at your best. Conversely, if you are revving too high when you need to be calmer, then you are not bringing the best version of yourself to the performance.

An example is when I was over-revving in my first ever knock-out game in the 50-Over World Cup in 2007. It was a semi-final against a great South African side in St Lucia. I desperately wanted to stand up in a big game as all of the great players always did, but I had never defined what intensity level I needed to be at my best. I totally over-revved through the whole bowling innings. I was just trying way too hard and I bowled nowhere near my best. I got away with it, because the team performed so well but it was a time I learnt from because I let myself get too overawed by the importance of the game and certainly didn't bring the best version of myself at that time.

There are a few great examples of players who deeply know their optimal level of intensity. The first one is Virat Kohli. When he is at his best, which is very visible, he is in the battle front and centre, every ball. Whereas AB de Villiers and Usman Khawaja are on the opposite end of the spectrum. Both of these guys get into their bubble and just stay there. They don't need to engage with anyone around them to find their optimum intensity zone. AB de Villiers never engaged with the bowler. He would always turn his back after every ball to not make eye contact with the bowler. He didn't need this intensity of the battle for him to be at his best.

Where is your zone?

In our optimal performance mindset, we need to clearly define the levels we need to be at so we can understand when we're in the sweet spot and when we're not. When we are at our best, in that 'zone' of best performance, there's always a blend of calm and intensity that coexist perfectly. It is possible to be emotionally calm but physically and mentally intense at the same time, and when we're able to hit this 'sweet spot', performing at a high level becomes somewhat effortless, even though we're potentially expending a great deal of energy.

Looking at the two tachometers should give you a good visual of where you are aiming. In terms of your calmness, what is your optimal level, if 0 is asleep and 10 is freaking out or being super anxious?

For me, it was between 2.5 and 3.5 on the 'calm' dial. That level would fit with my best. It meant I wasn't asleep or sluggish at 0 or 1. I didn't want to be ultra-relaxed or super chilled. I definitely didn't want to move it above 3.5 or even above 4. Because it meant that I started to burn too much mental energy when I didn't need to.

And on the intensity tachometer, 0 means you literally don't care, you are super lethargic, and 10 means you are over-revving and going absolutely manic.

For me, when I was at my best from a cricket perspective, I was probably around 8 to 8.5 on the 'intense' dial. Because for me to be my best I needed to be in a battle. I needed to have my intensity right up, me against them. I needed to be pushing up towards 8.5 to be at my absolute best. If I went down to around 5 or 6, I was much more susceptible to a poor performance because I would go more internal and battle with myself, rather than thinking external and having the battle with the bowler or someone in the field. It didn't have to be verbal. It could be an internal battle between me and one of the players on the ground that they didn't even know about. Or it could be a battle off the field, trying to prove someone wrong. I had to pick a fight with someone and direct my intensity towards them otherwise I would be more susceptible when I turned that intensity on myself. This is mentally very challenging, to get yourself up for the battle every time and find the intensity that you need when you are at your absolute best. Some days, I found it really difficult to find that battle. But after a game where I knew that I didn't find the intensity level that I needed to perform at my best, and I had a not so good game, then I sat back and would say to myself, 'What is more important? Pushing myself to find the intensity that I need to give myself the best chance of having a great game? Or feeling like crap, like I do now?' I knew I had to push myself into that intensity zone to be at my best, otherwise I would not bring out my best performance.

KEY TAKEAWAYS

- Everyone has their own optimal calmness and intensity when they are at their absolute best.
- You need to define what yours is so that you know what you are chasing in the lead-up to and during your performance.

Aim small to miss small

We need to be very specific in what part of your life you want to define your ACT Model around. If we define something very specific, we have more chance of success than if we are very broad. We can miss if we aim too broadly because we don't know what we're aiming for. A sniper, a sharpshooter, aims very small. They pick a really small target to aim for so if they miss, they miss small. So pick an aspect of your life that you want to bring the best version of yourself and define your ACT Model around this. We can have a number of different ACT Models depending on different parts of your life. At the core, they are often similar but there may be different attributes at play depending on what part of your life you choose. My ACT Model for my cricket-playing days is very different to my ACT Model for being the best version of myself as a father. Because if I brought my cricket-playing ACT Model into being the best dad I could be, well, I might be in jail as you will understand when you see what my ACT Model for me as a cricketer was.

The ACT Model

The word ACT is an acronym. The A refers to your A-game attributes. These are the words that define you when you are at your absolute best. C refers to the process of critique where you compare your desired A attribute to how you performed on the day. This is an important part of the process that I will explain in detail. T refers to the process of transformation that is achieved through self-talk. This is the final key element to the ACT Model, and is the key ingredient responsible for reprogramming your unconscious mind to bring the best version of yourself to every single performance.

What does excellence look like for you? We need to deeply define exactly what it looks like and feels like from a mental perspective – for you. Because once you deeply define it you know exactly what it looks like and what you are chasing every time you step out to perform. You know which way you are trying to move the pendulum. But if you never define it, which I never did up until this point, you don't know what you're chasing every time you step out. During my Test career, I knew what I was trying to do technically, in terms of batting, bowling and fielding skills. But from an intensity and mental perspective, in terms of creating the right mental environment for my technical skills to flourish, I didn't know what that looked like.

Sometimes I would fall into the right mental state if someone engaged with me on the field and got me into a battle so that my battle was outward. That was when I was at my best unless I went too far the other way. And when I was younger I would sometimes get too engaged in the battle and start to lose the plot, which meant I was nowhere near my best.

Opening the batting pushed me into the right mindset

Up until the end of 2015, there were numerous circumstances throughout my international career that allowed me to fall into my best performance mindset. Most of the time it was a battle on the field or something off the field that caused me to get a bee in my bonnet. I would want to prove someone wrong and that pushed me into my best performance mindset. This meant that I was right up for the contest and I had a laser focus on winning the battle to come out on top.

But then there was the other mindset that came about because of the circumstances in my life and this mindset was the 'celebration mode' mindset, where I felt like all of the shackles came off and I was able to just take the game on without any fear or worry about the consequences. This came about after a build-up over nearly four years of being constantly injured to a point where I thought that my dream of playing for Australia and winning games off my own bat was just about over. I had a tough year in 2007 as I was rebuilding my body in an attempt to become more resilient to handle the rigours of being a fast/medium bowling allrounder playing international cricket. Then after my successful inaugural IPL in 2008, my mindset shifted to celebration mode, just enjoying every moment of being out on the field and taking the game on, as I couldn't believe that I was doing what I was doing. I was opening the batting in ODI and T20I cricket for Australia and scoring runs against the best bowlers in the world, which then led to an opportunity to open the batting in Test cricket during the 2009 Ashes series. And then my game just took off! I started to bat in a way that I only ever dreamed of and this was all because I had no fear from ball one. I let go of all of that care and pressure that I had been putting on myself and just took the bowlers on from ball one in every format that I was batting in.

Once I started to open the batting, my mindset shifted in two ways. The first one was that circumstances over the previous four years with my injuries had allowed me to let go of the results and just enjoy the moment of playing. I was celebrating being out there. Everything else was a bonus. The second one, which was equally as powerful, was that opening the batting had made me let go of the situation and the results that had previously led to me tying myself into knots. I had previously been batting at No.3 or No.4 in first-class cricket or No.6 in Test cricket, where my mindset was totally dictated by the situation when I went in to bat. If we were 4 for 40 and in trouble, my mindset would be, 'Don't get out, let's build an innings and a partnership with my mate, now is not a good time to get out.' Or if we were 4 for 300, my mindset would be, 'This is a T20 and I am going to just take them down,' which was higher risk batting that very rarely worked out for me at that time. But opening the batting had shifted my mind to a place where I didn't care if I got out because I was setting the platform for the team and if I got out, the rest of the guys had to pick up the pieces. The freedom that this gave me every time I went out to bat was amazing. It was always the same situation, 0 for 0, and I was one of the ones who could help set the game up for my team. This made me let go of caring about the outcomes and I had the simple mindset of trying to take the bowlers down, whether that be in T20 cricket, One-Day cricket or Test cricket.

This coincided with my most successful period of batting in international cricket over a two-year period where I scored runs consistently in all formats of the game. Then as soon as I moved back down the order, I didn't have the understanding of how to recreate this 'celebration mode mindset' and the 'fearless opening batting mindset' where I didn't care if I got out. The self-inflicted pressure started to build again over the next few years and my performances started to be much more inconsistent.

What I now know is these two circumstances made me fall into my optimum performance mindset, which was so bloody powerful and it was no surprise why I had such an incredibly successful period. But because I didn't know what or why this mindset worked so well for me, it wasn't until I got educated on what my optimum mindset was by deeply defining the best version of me, that I finally realised what the best version of me was and the exact mindset that I should be chasing every time I went out to play!

16

Your A-game Attributes

The first step in the ACT Model process is for you to define your A-game attributes. You do this by taking your mind back to your very best performance, the one moment or performance you would love to recreate every time. It is that moment where you had that performance you always dreamed about. The one that you had worked so hard for and made so many sacrifices for. Now imagine there is a magic camera hovering around you with the ability to see you both externally and internally. We touched on this earlier regarding imagery. The camera can see your body language, your demeanour, and your presence. But it can also go inside your mind as well and it sees and hears what you were saying about yourself and what you were thinking at the very moment in time during that performance when you were at your absolute best.

WHAT WOULD YOUR MAGIC CAMERA SEE?

What are the things that the magic camera would show you? What are the words that would describe you on that day of personal virtuosity? Start to write them down. What would your teammates or your opposition have said about you on that day? Take your mind back to that moment. Where did that performance occur? What time of year was it? What was the weather like that day? What time of day did that performance occur? Also, in the lead-up to that moment, what were the circumstances like? Was there anything that stands out to you in the lead-up to this day that helped direct your mind to where it was on that day?

Take the time right now to brainstorm the words that described you during that performance. Write down any word that comes to mind. There are no wrong words or answers here. These are your words. It generally takes 15–20 minutes to work through this process. What you are actually doing is creating a very powerful mind-map of exactly what you look like when you are at your absolute best.

To give you some examples of common A-game attributes, when people are defining the best version of themselves, here are the general themes with some common adjectives around it.

- **calm**; relaxed; loose; cool; rested; at peace; detached; unflappable; in harmony; comfortable; composed; free; heavy; breathe; fulfilled; serene; tranquil; chill; secure; grateful; quiet; blissful; emotionless; neutral
- **focused**; here and now; single-minded; in my shell; clear-headed; centred; sharp; tuned-in; alert; in the moment; non-judgmental; fully present; locked in; connected; zeroed in; clairvoyant; issue at hand; alone; head up
- **confident**; arrogant; bullet-proof; powerful; strong; walking tall; cocky; dominant; positive; self-assured; believe; connected; courageous; bold; well-prepared; capable; invincible; committed; superior; the one; empowered; chest out; trust; certain; no doubt

- **energised**; pumped-up; revved-up; passionate; joyful; challenged; enthusiastic; fun; excited; motivated; alive

- **aggressive**; tenacious; persistent; intense; unstoppable; hungry; on the edge; assertive; predator; purposeful; relentless; decisive; panther; lion; shark; dedicated; determined; fearless; pushing the limit; alpha

- **smooth**; rhythm; fluid; flow; effortless; easy; nimble; tempo; slow motion; efficient

- **anticipate**; analytical; opportunistic; adaptable; smart; adaptive; flawless; sensitive; calculating; open-minded; flexible; aware; cunning

- **in control**; in command; measured; selfish; patient; professional; responsible; inspiring; precise; methodical; deliberate; persuasive; manipulating; Machiavellian; chameleon; leader; balanced; poised; take charge; convincing; accurate

So now that you have spent the time to define your A-game attributes, stop for a moment and think about how you feel right now? What you should feel is more like that person at that moment in time when you had that performance of your life. It feels pretty good, right! And this is the incredible power of the ACT Model. When we work our way through the ACT Model before every training session, and every game day, we are pulling ourselves into the mindset of this best version of ourselves. We feel this way and guess what, the unconscious mind, the crew of the ship says, 'Aye aye captain, I have got this, I can take you right there!'

In other words, the ACT Model serves as the rudder-control process of the conscious mind to powerfully direct your unconscious mind. That's the power of imagery. Making the most of the power that we have to unconsciously move that pendulum in the right direction.

Grouping attributes

Now that you have written down all of the attributes that describe you during that day of your own personal virtuosity, you need to start to work through grouping these attributes together. You do this by seeing if there are some words that mean a similar thing along the lines of the various examples of words that you have read through previously. For example, if 'confident' is one of the words that you've written down, as well as 'bullet-proof' or 'chest out', group these words together under the heading of 'confident'. Do this to all of the attributes that you've written down. If there are a few words that are along similar lines to 'calm', group these together under 'calm'.

Once you have gone through this process, it should look a little like this below.

CALM	CORRECT FOCUS
REACTING	AGGRESSIVE

Now that you have grouped your attributes together, the next step is to identify the most powerful words that you have written down. These will be the ones that mean the most to you. The ones that stand out the most and that described you the best during that amazing performance that you wish you could replicate every time you go out to play. When I was working through this process, I had two words in and around 'focus' that I had written down. The first one was 'correct focus' and the other one was 'be on'. The most powerful one for me was 'correct focus' as it really meant to stay totally present so that I knew which skill of focus I needed right at that moment in time, whereas 'be on' was a little more broad, so it was not as powerful.

The words that I arrived at when I defined my ACT Model were 'calm', 'correct focus', 'smart', 'reacting', 'feeling arrogant' and 'aggressive'. I'll explain further how I arrived at those in detail.

Finalising your ACT Model

After you have grouped all of your attributes together and have identified which attribute out of each group stands out the most to you and has the most power, the next step is to work through the progression of thought in the ACT Model, which is vitally important to get the best result from this process.

The first word in your ACT Model is normally around a state of calmness or contentment, a chilled state of mind. Or it can also be around the pure fun, joy and excitement of playing the game that we all love. The theme of fun is normally the centrepiece of a lot of people's ACT Model. The pure joy and excitement of doing what you love, to let go and just have fun, is such an important thread for most of us when we are at our absolute best.

I know I certainly didn't do my best work when I was worried or anxious about the performance that was coming up.

The next word in your ACT Model normally has a focus aspect to it, which for me was around being correctly focused.

The third word in your ACT Model normally has an element of trusting what you feel, or trusting your instincts or your best decision-making strategy when you are performing at your best, or how you tap into your unconscious mind for skill execution, like 'smooth' or 'reacting' for example.

The next two words are always around your confidence and, with this, the intensity that you had during that incredible day that you have defined your ACT Model on.

The last word, which is the most powerful, is normally an action or doing word. It can be a state of mind that, if all else fails, if I am not calm, if I am not trusting my gut, if I am not focused correctly, if my confidence is a little off right at that moment in time, I can jam this word into my mind, and I am right there at my absolute best. For me this word was 'aggressive'. I knew that if I jammed this word into my head as the ball was delivered, I was going to override everything and get out of my own way to be at my best. Other common final words that cricketer's have used in their ACT Models that I have been a part of developing are 'fearless', and for a couple of bowlers, the word 'length' was their 'doing' word. If all else failed, they put those words into their mind at the right time, and they will be right where they need to be.

Floor plan

The ACT Model isn't a checklist. It's not a set of words you remind yourself of occasionally and do the mental equivalent of ticking the box. It is an incredibly powerful process where the words of your ACT Model serve as portals to direct your dominant thought to reflect on the memories, images and feelings associated with that one attribute you had on that day of virtuosity.

We can use the simple analogy of the floorplan of a house to visualise the ACT Model and provide more depth and context to every one of your very powerful attributes. Imagine that each room of the house has a door that we have to open to step into. And on that door is a big sign with one of the attributes of your ACT Model.

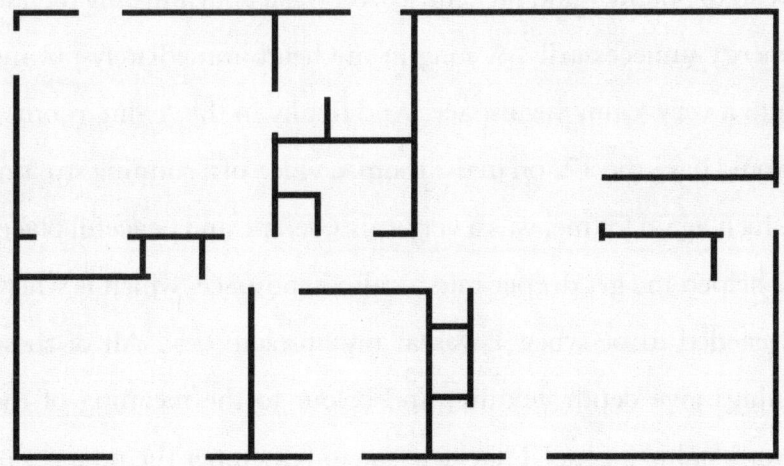

Now I want you to imagine walking into that room and I want you to fill out that room with various things that add much more depth to that attribute. Let me talk through what my room looked like when I was filling out my 'calm' room, to give more depth and context to the word.

As I was standing outside the room, I was thinking about exactly what 'calm' represented for me when I had that day that I always was dreaming about having. The one word that I would have in big writing on the wall inside the room was 'serene', as this put me straight into a very calm, tranquil head space. And with this, I then had a painting of a rainforest, which for me is such a peaceful place. In this room I would have a speaker on, playing my favourite songs. As soon as I think of the word 'calm', straight away I think of putting/jamming a song into my head to put my mind on neutral, so I wasn't burning any mental energy unnecessarily. A song in my head immediately put me into a very 'calm' headspace. And finally in this 'calm' room, I would have the TV on in the room, a video of a running stream, which again for me, was a very calm, serene and peaceful place. It helped me get deeper into a calm headspace, which is where I needed to be when I was at my absolute best. All of these things give depth, texture, and colour to the meaning of the word 'calm' for me. They help me to remember the nuances of what 'calm' felt like when I was at my absolute best.

Work through this for yourself with every attribute in your ACT Model to give these individual words or phrases much more depth and meaning.

Once you are done filling out all of these rooms in your floor plan of your ACT Model, the power comes when you visualise walking into every room, one by one in your specific ACT Model order until you get to the end of the floor plan. This progression of thought immediately turns you from the normal version of you as you step into the first room, to the super version of you once you come out of the last room. All of a sudden we feel and become that very version of ourselves that we were on our very best day. That's the person you want to be when you step out onto the field for your next game. We have provided our conscious mind with the imagery necessary to control the rudder to direct ourselves into the unconscious mind, which is where all of our best performances sit.

17

My ACT Model and How I Defined It

I'll now explain how I came up with my ACT Model. I based it on an IPL game in May 2015, just a few months before I met Jacques.

I was playing for Rajasthan Royals and it was a knockout game against Kolkata in Mumbai. If we lost, then we were out, and if we won, we would qualify for the finals. A win would also ensure we qualified for the Champions League, which was a huge financial windfall for the franchise. There were a few things that went down that season in the lead-up to the game. I was captain at the start of the season, and I got injured and missed the first four games. Steve Smith was captain for those first four games, and Rajasthan won them all.

Then I came back from injury and, just as I was about to play my first game, I got called into a meeting with the coaches. They had concerns about my fitness and they were interested in keeping Steve as captain if I was open to it. I wanted to play and be captain. I had never had the opportunity to captain a team before as I had always been the young guy in my team and, as an allrounder, I had a fair bit on my plate. Captaincy wasn't something that teams wanted to lump on me. I always wanted to take on a captaincy role to see how good I could be as the main leader on the field. I had learned so much from some of the greatest captains that had ever played. Ricky Ponting and Shane Warne were two incredible captains who I'd learned from. I felt like this was now my opportunity with the Rajasthan Royals after being there for six seasons. So I did continue on as captain for a few games but I ended up stepping down from the captaincy towards the back end of that season. Every time the team lost I could sense the pressure continuing to build, so it was time to relinquish the role. I felt like I didn't need the unnecessary scrutiny in my life.

So, I had a big point to prove. I also hadn't had the best season from a performance perspective leading into this specific game. But this game was just the perfect storm in so many ways. My preparation was as perfect as I could have planned out. We had a few days off in the lead-up to this game, so I was able to prepare exactly how I wanted to with my batting. I was hitting the ball exactly how I wanted to be. I was able to work on what I needed to bowling-wise as well. My best preparation meant that I had ticked off my power hitting by doing some range hitting. I knew deep down I was getting into the perfect positions for me to power any ball in my zone over the fence. And from a bowling perspective, I had a free net without a batter to practise all of my variations without the worry of the ball being smashed back at me, which meant I could have the single focus on my skill and execution without the fear of wearing one in my follow through.

And I had a bee in my bonnet. That was the mindset I took into the game. I was just where I needed to be. I didn't get into a battle with the opposition. But internally, I had a big point to prove. It was the battle that I needed to be at my best. I ended up nearly single-handedly winning this knockout game for the Rajasthan Royals to get us through to the finals and into the Champions League. I scored 104 not out from 59 balls and took 2 for 38 from 4 overs.

If the magic camera was on me for that game, it would have shown that I had a real calmness about me because of my preparation. I knew my game was where it needed to be. As I walked out to bat, I was very much at peace with where my game was at right there and then.

The second thing I could see is that I was correctly focused. I was focused on what I needed to do at that moment in time. I wasn't revving too high, but I was just where I needed to be. I was watching the ball like a hawk as the bowler was releasing the ball and then in between balls, I was calm, ready to get back into the fight again.

The third thing the camera saw was that I was using my cricket smarts. In other words, I was trusting what I felt. I was trusting my gut. I was making the most of the experience that I had and fully committing to what I felt. I was not second guessing myself at all and I had no fear whatsoever!

The fourth thing the camera saw was me totally reacting to what was coming down at me.

I hardly premeditated at all, and if I did, I pulled myself back straightaway. If I ever did premeditate, it meant I was out of position or I was just hoping they would bowl in the right area, and that wasn't me at my best. The only shot I did premeditate was a lap sweep, which needs to be premeditated as a tactical shot. But it was a tactical premeditation that I committed to fully.

Premeditation

Before I go any further, it is important to understand premeditation for batters. It is very dangerous. It was for me and I always see it with other batters. Premeditation is needed for lap sweeps, reverse sweeps, and switch hits in particular, but when I see a batter premeditating for other strokes outside of these shots, it means that if the bowler doesn't bowl it right where the batter wants it to be bowled, they are totally out of position. This means that you could be missing out on other scoring opportunities compared to just standing still and reacting to the ball coming down.

I had to fight this urge, especially under pressure when I needed to find a boundary. But deep down I knew that when I was at my absolute best, I was technically very neutral. This meant I had access to all shots around the ground. I would be aiming straight down the ground to ensure my technical alignment was right and then with the aggressive mindset, I would just react to the ball coming down, allowing the bowler to make a mistake. Whether it was a wide, full ball for me to hit through the off side or a shorter slower ball, I was ready to pounce on anything that the bowler bowled. The whole concept is around allowing a bowler to make a mistake and bowl a loose ball instead of trying to create one, which is very high risk. If you guess wrong, you will be out of position, which means more chance of getting out.

I have worked with one of the best short format batters in the world and, after opening the batting with him in one of the big T20 tournaments, I could see at various times during an over that he would premeditate one area where he would be aiming to hit the ball, no matter where the ball was bowled. He would charge down the wicket and just look to be hitting it through the covers and towards point. When it wasn't bowled in the perfect spot for that shot he was out of position. He risked getting out so often and needed so much luck to survive because the ball wasn't exactly where he had predicted. This guy is one of the most talented batters who has played over the last 10 years and has all of the shots, all around the ground, whether it's against quicks or spin. In all types of conditions he can hit the ball to all parts of the ground. Once he understood that it was OK to premeditate charging down the track, but not premediating the area he was going to hit the ball, all of a sudden by aiming straight and staying more neutral he had access to hitting the ball to all parts of the ground depending on where the bowler bowled it. This helped him in a big way. He didn't miss out on loose balls that a bowler bowled and also played with much less risk while having even more scoring options available to him.

But most batters when they are under pressure to score start to premeditate only hitting to one area. Once they catch that thought and redirect it to trusting their instincts and muscle memory, all of a sudden they pull themselves into the best version of themselves, where they have all of the shots that they have practised at their disposal, and available on command.

KEY TAKEAWAYS

- We need to set ourselves up every ball to allow our instincts to take over and allow the bowler to bowl a loose ball.
- There are premeditated shots that are predominantly tactical options and need to be fully committed to.
- If we try to predict where the ball is going to be bowled, if the ball is not exactly there, we are totally out of position and we give the bowler a better chance of getting us out.

The last two attributes of my ACT Model

The fifth attribute I defined during this innings for Rajasthan was being internally arrogant. My attitude was, 'I'm here, I'm going to show you guys how good I am and I am going to take you guys down.' I showed it in my body language because I was in the battle, and I had the right intensity.

The ACT Model can be ever-evolving as well, as I didn't actually realise how important the level of intensity was at the

time when I defined it initially. In this game, I had the 'f***
you' attitude deep inside me as I was proving a point due to
the circumstances surrounding that game. The intensity in
this outward battle was the place that I needed to get to for
me to be at my absolute best. And as I look back, not just at
that moment in time, but at other times in my career when
I had a great game, I had that intensity and attitude in me
whether it was from an external factor in the lead-up to the
game, or whether it was in the game where someone had a go
at me and I got into the battle straight away. I was not battling
myself internally at all. All of my energy was outward with
my back against the wall to really prove a point that I was not
going to be beaten. My senses, my reflexes, everything was
heightened to the point that I was ready to go every ball. So
the internally arrogant attribute evolved to 'f*** you' in my
ACT Model.

The last thing this magic camera saw was that I was
aggressive. That's me at my best, when I'm being aggressive
and I'm reacting fast. And because of rule number 2, the word
'aggressive' was the right thing I needed to put into my mind at
the right time. So in the worst-case scenario, if all those other
attributes weren't there, I would put 'aggressive' into my mind,
and it took me right to that place that I needed to be when I
was at my best.

Sure enough, with all those attributes on display, I delivered one of my very best performances and we won by nine runs.

When I defined my ACT Model using this game, there was a number of attributes that I wrote down around these general themes but these six attributes: 'calm', 'correct focus', 'smart', 'reacting', 'feeling arrogant', and 'aggressive' were the ones that had the most potency and had the most meaning for me at that very moment in time.

My ACT Model

1. Calm
2. Correct focus
3. Smart
4. Reacting
5. Feeling arrogant / 'f*** you'
6. Aggressive

KEY TAKEAWAYS

- We need to pick one specific part of our life to define our ACT Model, as we have different ones for different parts of our lives.
- Defining your powerful attributes as the super version of yourself means that you know what you are chasing every time you go out to perform.

- Filling out the floor plan gives even more depth and context for each attribute to build that deeper connection with every single one.
- With practice, we can step through our ACT Model and turn from Clark Kent into Superman in an instant.

18

Compare – The Value of Self-Critique

It's very important to understand the difference between critique and criticism, and also the honesty part around it.

Critiquing is assessing things unemotionally without the value judgement that exists in a criticism. It is when you reflect on a performance and identify where it didn't go right or didn't go exactly to plan. It's not about beating yourself up over a failure or a bad game, but rather understanding what you didn't do as well as you could have and learning from it for the next time this situation arises. Using this simple method of critique, you can then devise a plan to do things differently next time to hopefully get a better outcome.

Criticism has a judgement aspect to it. It's like telling yourself, 'You're junk! What the hell was that? You're weak! You're soft! You are a loser!'

How many times have you heard that type of criticism in sporting environments? 'You guys were rubbish today. What were you thinking? You guys are better than that!! You're soft! You're weak!'

We've all heard those things before from coaches or players in those environments and you may have even said them to yourself, as I did.

But criticism moves you to start to dig a bigger hole, which can be very difficult to get out of and it moves you further away from the mindset that you need to have to be at your best.

What is important to understand about the difference between critiquing and criticism, is that critiquing is not meant to produce false positives. It's not about letting yourself off the hook and blowing smoke or inventing excuses. It is about being clinical and unemotional in assessing what didn't exactly go to plan and then identifying what things to put in place to be able to do it better next time and limit the chances of making these mistakes again.

The other important aspect is the honesty around it. Just because you have had a great result, it doesn't necessarily mean you have brought the best version of yourself. And vice versa, just because the result wasn't great, that doesn't mean you didn't bring the best version of yourself. Critiquing is just assessing things honestly with the Performance Equation in mind. Sometimes you will have a great result or outcome, but you will need to identify that a number of B factors went your way. You might identify that you made a number of mistakes and got away with them. In that assessment, you will need to work out how to do things better next time so that you limit the mistakes and increase your chances of getting the result without relying on the B factors to help you, as those positive B factors won't be there every time for you, because as we know, they are out of your control.

The language around critiquing and criticism is incredibly important.

Criticism can have judgement and severe negative connotations and consequences. Critiquing in the right way will be beneficial in terms of finding solutions and getting better in the long run. Critiquing should be welcomed in every environment and should be every player's responsibility, but criticism should never ever be allowed.

Building your growth mindset using self-critique

Once we've defined the attributes of our ACT Model based on our best ever performance we can then reshape our thinking.

Once you have completed any performance, you need to take time to evaluate how well you did compared to the attributes you have defined yourself by. In this self-critique, you need to compare the behaviours and mindset that you had during the performance or the game you have just played against your A-game attributes. You answer the simple question: 'How did I do in that moment of performance, relative to my A game standard for that attribute?'

A journal is a really good resource to give structure to this systematic self-analysis process. I used a journal throughout my career, but I used it much more efficiently and clinically in terms of critiquing my performances after deeply defining my ACT Model. I have included a blank self-critiquing sheet that you can photocopy for your daily critique and I have also provided an example of one that I filled out after one performance.

With the ACT Model, it's about doing it every day and performing a GAP analysis (Good, Average, Poor). You have defined your A-game attributes and then every single day when you've played or trained, or whatever it is you are doing, you compare and critique it against when you are at your absolute best.

When you start comparing and critiquing on a daily basis, that's when you start to build much better mental skill habits.

This means moving into a growth mindset, which is the ultimate mindset that we are chasing to override our old habits and create new high-performance habits.

The question you need to ask yourself is, 'Was I 10 out of 10 with this attribute today?' A 10 out of 10 score would be when you were exactly matching the attributes that you have defined your ACT Model around. Then the honest critique kicks in. 'I was probably only 7 out of 10 today.'

KEY TAKEAWAYS

- Critiquing assesses the outcome with no value judgement whatsoever. It is all about where did it go wrong and how can I do it better next time to give myself the best chance of getting a better result – the Growth Mindset.

- Criticism is assessing the outcome with a value judgement attached to it, which is destructive and has no positive impact in any way.

- Doing a GAP analysis after every performance, whether that be in training or in game, will speed up your development to be able to turn on the super version of you and stay there at will.

PERSONAL ACT MODEL
CRITIQUE LOG BOOK

DATE: EVENT:

PERSONAL ACT MODEL ATTRIBUTES	POOR	IDEAL
MY PERSONAL PERFORMANCE	1 - 2 - 3 - 4 - 5 - 6 - 7 - 8 - 9	
	1 - 2 - 3 - 4 - 5 - 6 - 7 - 8 - 9	
	1 - 2 - 3 - 4 - 5 - 6 - 7 - 8 - 9	
	1 - 2 - 3 - 4 - 5 - 6 - 7 - 8 - 9	
	1 - 2 - 3 - 4 - 5 - 6 - 7 - 8 - 9	
	1 - 2 - 3 - 4 - 5 - 6 - 7 - 8 - 9	
	1 - 2 - 3 - 4 - 5 - 6 - 7 - 8 - 9	

PROBLEMS (THE ONLY SPACE I'M ALLOWED TO SUMMARISE THE NEGATIVES):

PERSONAL ACT MODEL™
PERFORMANCE LOG BOOK

DATE: 21/11/15   EVENT: Grade Cricket

PERSONAL ACT MODEL™ STANDARDS OF EXCELLENCE

	POOR								IDEAL
My personal performance	1 - 2 - 3 - 4 - 5 - 6 -(6.5)- 7 - 8 - 9								
Calm	1 - 2 - 3 - 4 - 5 - 6 - 7 -(7.5)- 8 - 9								
Correct focus	1 - 2 - 3 - 4 - 5 -(6)- 7 - 8 - 9								
Smart	1 - 2 - 3 - 4 - 5 - 6 -(7)- 8 - 9								
Reacting	1 - 2 - 3 - 4 - 5 -(6)- 7 - 8 - 9								
Feel Arrogant	1 - 2 - 3 - 4 - 5 - 6 -(7)- 8 - 9								
Aggressive	1 - 2 - 3 - 4 - 5 - 6 -(6.5)- 7 - 8 - 9								

Problems (the only space I'm allowed to summarise the negatives):

- My focus was not always correct. It was a long day in the field but I need to challenge myself to practice my mental routine every ball so when my batting comes along, I have already been working on this routine.

- Reacting → Wasn't in the moment consistently.

Solutions Box (where I write about solutions and how I want to be):

Calm - Not bad apart from running late today which got me worked up. Need to sort this out so it doesn't happen again.

Correct Focus - Need to practice my mental routine so I tune out in between balls but then get my mental & technical routine down pat but already been working on refining H. Need to get to work on really developing these routines. ✓

Smart - Not too bad today. Need to get into the game again but need to really use my cricket smarts & smarts in general to be at my best.

Reacting - Needed to be more in the moment today. Talking a bit too much so didn't get my routine down pat, so that I was just reacting aggressively. ✓

Feel Arrogant - Pretty good today. keep feeling 'Be The Man', 'Chest Out', - Make bowler feel pressure with my body language so they shit themselves.

Aggressive - Needed to be more aggressive in the field, but for batting not too bad at the start. With my dominant thought. I am in control of my dominant thought. ✓

Transform – use self-talk

Then we move into the T of the ACT Model. The T stands for Transform, or more specifically, self-talk to transform or morph yourself into this person defined by your A-game attributes, to imagine or picture the shift in thinking. Essentially it is the internal dialogue to make sure the pendulum is moving in the right direction to bring the best version of yourself to your performance.

If you were 7 out of 10 in an attribute after critiquing your performance, then the transformation process needs to happen. Where was I slightly off today? Where did it start to shift? Once I identify that, I know that next time if I start to go in that direction again, I can redirect myself to where I need to go.

If you work through the ACT Model correctly you will be able to transform from Clark Kent into Superman within seconds. You are moving the rudder in the right direction and the unconscious mind crew says, 'Yep I've got it, I'll take you there.'

Every time I went out to play and to practise later in my career, I would step through my ACT Model and engage my self-talk. I would step through every word. I would write it in my diary before the game or training and then repeat the process before every ball during the game. With the word 'calm', I'd write down associated words like 'serene' and 'tranquil'. With 'correct focus' I'd write down the various stages of correct focus I needed, from being 'broad', to 'watching the ball', to 'pulling back', to 'song in my head'.

Then in the performance, while I was batting, I would run through the ACT Model quickly between balls and critique myself after each ball. I would ask myself, 'was I correctly focused for that ball? Did I premeditate, or was I reacting? Was I trusting my gut? Am I in the battle? Have I put the word aggressive in my head at the right time?' I was flying through that checklist every ball.

It seems like overload at first. But the more I did it and the more I practised it, I became superefficient at working through it after every ball. During my pre-game routine, I would meditate before I left for the game to replenish the mental energy that I had already used up to that point. This included the mental energy that I had burnt in working through my 45 minutes of preparation time for the game. In game, at the non-striker's end, I would switch off and jam a song in my head to conserve my mental energy. Post-game, or post-performance, I would isolate my critiquing to a very short space of time. I would be clinical with the questions I asked myself and how I reviewed my ACT Model, and then once I had done that, I would move on.

This is the key to the whole process to transform your thinking and bring the best version of you to every performance.

KEY TAKEAWAYS

- Self-talk gives you the power to control the internal dialogue to transform yourself into the super version of yourself.

The power of a team ACT Model

All throughout the ACT Model process, I've mentioned that you need to deeply define the best version of you so that you know what you are chasing every time you go out to play. This process is also ridiculously powerful if you do this as a team or leadership group too. Imagine sitting down as a team after one of those team performances that you always dream about being a part of, and deeply defining everything around that performance, from the lead-up to the game itself. Then collectively, every time you all walk out on the field, you all have a deep understanding of what the A-game attributes look like when your team is at its absolute best. And every moment of every game, in the lead-up, during and after the game, you all collectively exhibit this version of the group. This team ACT Model will set very clearly defined A-game attributes that everyone knows this team needs to exhibit every time they step out onto the field. Yes, we all have our own individual ACT Model that we are bringing to every performance to pull ourselves into 'the zone'. But by having a team ACT Model, collectively the team will have the deep foundations of the super version of the team to always fall back on and critique after every game, which will help the team get closer and closer to consistently producing those team performances that we all dream about being a part of.

There is a big difference between doing a values session compared to defining the team ACT Model. I have sat through numerous team values sessions, attempting to come up with words that define what the team stands for. And yes, in the end these were only words no matter how much we all wanted these to turn into the standard behaviours within the team. But a team ACT Model is actually deeply defining what that amazing team performance looked like with the team A-game attributes. Then with daily critiquing around training and game days, this will build that growth mindset for the team to continue to push the limits to pull the team into that super team mindset much more consistently.

19

Bringing It All Together

To tie all of this together, and give you a sense of how this entire mental process that I've explained can be applied successfully in a game situation, I want to walk you through one of my best ever performances in detail. It will hopefully help explain how I used all of the lessons Jacques taught me, and the mental skills I had developed over three years of practical application in the world's best T20 leagues, to get a great result.

I have already touched on the 2018 IPL final. But it was the perfect embodiment of applying all of my mental and technical skills together, over and over again, to bring my best A game to a highly pressurised situation, with tens of millions watching and an IPL trophy on the line. It was also an example of how I minimised some of the external B factors and benefitted from some outside my control, to get an amazing result and prove the performance equation.

The 2018 IPL final was the first time that it was really obvious that I had pulled myself into 'the zone'. The zone is all about bringing 90–95 per cent of your focus on the A factors, the things you are in control of, and then having a little bit of awareness on the result to ensure you are on track.

My performance in the 2018 IPL for the Chennai Super Kings against Sunrisers Hyderabad, and particularly my mental performance, was even more significant because of what happened two years earlier in the 2016 IPL final when I was playing for Royal Challengers Bangalore against Sunrisers.

We lost that 2016 final, and I had one of my worst performances ever. It was a disaster. Even though I felt like I was well prepared and like I was mentally where I needed to be, everything went wrong. I was one of the key bowlers for RCB in that game. I bowled one over in the powerplay, one in the middle overs and two at the death, including the 18th and 20th over, and I got absolutely smashed. I just couldn't execute my yorker to Ben Cutting, who kept hitting me onto the roof of the M. Chinnaswamy Stadium. Cutting hit me for four sixes and I finished with figures of 0 for 61 from four overs as Sunrisers made a mammoth 7 for 208.

One of the reasons I bowled so poorly in the 2016 final was because of a negative B factor that I just didn't overcome. For some unknown reason, the creaseline that night was a little bit dusty and my front foot kept slipping at the bowling crease. Because I was sliding and wasn't stable on my front leg, my attempted yorkers kept coming out too full. A couple were hip high full tosses and they disappeared. In the critique of my performance, I accepted that my execution was slightly off and I needed to practise that scenario to reduce that B factor. Because it would arise again, whether it was a wet wicket or a dry one, I needed to work on a way to combat slipping at the crease in practice to limit the chance of having those same execution problems in the game. That was definitely a moment that stood out to me from a bowling perspective where a negative B factor had been too influential on the result because I hadn't worked on the technical skill in my preparation to override it and make it a smaller negative, instead of a really big one.

Then batting wise, I was in at number five and came out to bat with us needing 61 from 37 with seven wickets in hand. We still had a chance to win the game and I got out to Mustafizur Rahman at the wrong time, trying to take on their best bowler when I didn't need to. That performance really hurt, knowing the impact I had on that game. I was one of the key bowlers and batting in a crucial middle order role and I just stuffed it for the whole team.

With that context, I had that underlying feeling of failure again bleeding into my preparation for the 2018 final for Chennai against the same opponent, Sunrisers. As I mentioned previously, the feeling of failure can be a driver in your preparation. But as I've stressed, you can't let it turn into a fear of failure for the result or outcome. There is a distinct difference between the two things. What I learned was that I needed to use that feeling of failure from the 2016 final to drive myself to get my preparation spot on, so I could bring the best A version of myself to the 2018 final.

It was so important then to get my routine right and be conscious of my mental energy. I was diligent in making sure I conserved it heading into that night.

I stuck to my tried and trusted pre-game routine, which I had honed to a fine art by this point in my career. I'd mentioned the ways I used to torment myself in the lead-up to big games during my international career, like Ashes Tests or World Cup matches. I would burn through mental energy thinking about those matches for days in the lead-up and be completely fried by the first ball.

In 2018, I stuck to my routine. I did not think about the final until two hours before the team bus left for the ground.

The first 45 minutes of those two hours was for all of my mental planning. I used my diary to walk through my technical checklist. At that time, I had a number of technical thoughts that I went through in sequence. These were things I would repeat in sequence between balls as a reminder to myself of what I needed to focus on. The first one was making sure my eyes were level in my stance as the bowler ran in. Number two was making sure that my bottom hand, my right hand, was loose on the bat. I did not want to be gripping tight. It meant that my bat swing was going through the line of the ball and I could access the off side as well as the leg side, which was important for when bowlers would go wide to me. If I gripped too tight with my bottom hand I struggled to hit through the off side. The third technical thought was to make sure I was dipping my front shoulder. Sometimes in my stance, my front shoulder could get too high and it would mean I would need to dip my shoulder late in my bat swing to generate power. If I dipped it early in my stance I was much more efficient and quicker with my movements. The fourth point was to time my pre-movement and my forward press correctly and this was better being early than too late. The fifth was to keep my hands moving. I didn't want them to be static because when the bat is static it is at its heaviest, whereas a moving bat is much lighter. And then as the ball was bowled I wanted my head to be dead still. I needed my head to be still to get that fine focus on the ball, to be able to watch the ball all the way out of the hand and right onto my bat. If I moved late and was moving around as the bowler released, then my focus on the ball was a bit blurred. So I wrote down all of those points in my diary as a reminder for how I wanted to use that checklist in between balls during the game.

I also used that 45 minutes to write down my mental checklist of 'calm', 'correct focus', 'smart', 'reacting', 'f*** you', and 'aggressive' and went through my ACT Model. I would go through the ACT Model floor plan in detail to visualise what the best version of me looked like and remind myself of the attributes I needed for the final.

I also used that 45 minutes to look at footage, both of my opponents and of myself at my best. I wasn't dissecting footage forensically. I had faced a lot of the Sunrisers bowlers. But I was watching in order to put some fresh information into my unconscious mind, so I could tap into it with my gut feel later that night. I then watched a couple of YouTube videos of a couple of innings where I batted at my best to get that 'view mode' imagery fired up of me at my absolute best to take that version of me into the game.

Once that 45 minutes was done, I would shut off my devices and close my diary. I didn't want to burn any more mental energy. I needed to re-energise over the next 50 minutes before we had to depart for the ground. I did this through a 30-minute yoga session. This was something that I incorporated into my routine later in my career after a conversation with 1987 Wimbledon champion Pat Cash. Early in my career I'd been told not to stretch, as there was a thought at the time from some of the medical practitioners who I worked with that over-stretching was a bad thing. Cash, like so many great tennis players, knew the opposite was true for older athletes and that we needed more elasticity later in our careers to avoid injury. It made perfect sense. So I made sure I did 30 minutes of yoga. I then did 20 minutes of meditation. This period was vitally important. I needed to regenerate the mental energy that I had burned in the 45 minutes of working through my technical and mental thoughts. Those 20-minute meditations reset my mental energy stores and freshened my mind for the upcoming game.

Having stuck to my routine ahead of the 2018 IPL final, I was well prepared to handle what was to come. Chennai bowled first. I did not bowl in the final. We had four specialist bowlers plus two other allrounders in Dwayne Bravo and Ravindra Jadeja to bowl the overs. My job was to open the batting, a role that gave me the freedom that I needed to be at my best.

We were chasing 179 to win. I was not thinking about the target, or the pressure of the situation. I was just trying to pull myself into the zone by going through my technical and mental checklist in between balls. Every single ball I would go through my sequence of thoughts rapid fire. I would check my mental cues, 'calm, correct focus, smart, reacting, f*** you, and aggressive'. Then as the bowler was running in I would check my technical cues in order, 'eyes level, loose bottom hand, dip front shoulder, pre-movement, hands moving, head dead still'. The last thing I jammed into my head at the release of the ball was 'aggressive'. Then when I needed to switch off in between balls I jammed a song in my head to keep my mind on neutral. I was following the rules of the mental road. I remember that in a couple of deliveries in the first few overs some technical things were off. One delivery I was a little bit closed-off in my pre-movement and I was too far off side of the ball. I was able to check that in my list in between deliveries and ensure that I was neutral with my pre-movement and not committing too much to the off side. There was another ball where I felt a little bit rushed. My pre-movement had been a little bit late and my eyes were moving as the ball came out of the bowler's hand.

This technical checklist might seem like it's complicated in between balls. But because it was a routine of thought, something that I had practised over and over again, processing that information didn't take much time or burn too much mental energy at all.

My mental checklist was more simple, and I would then jam a song in my head to put my mind on neutral in between balls and trust what I felt. It was important to have the song in my head to access my gut feel on this night. Bhuvneshwar Kumar was bowling well for Sunrisers in the first few overs and the ball was swinging quite a lot and late, so I was trusting my gut and trusting my skill. But the other thing I needed to do was to make sure the word 'aggressive' was in my head at the right time. I remember the fifth ball from Bhuvi in the first over of the chase was short and wide and I missed out, fluffing a cut shot straight to the point fielder.

After that ball I immediately identified that I was a tiny bit hesitant, because the ball was swinging. That aggressive intent that I wanted, trusting my gut to go at the ball in a powerful position, was slightly off. With the ball swinging, I had leant towards being more defensive just to get through that over while the ball was moving around. After that one ball, I said to myself, 'No, I need to be aggressive and trust my instincts. If the ball swings, my skill is going to take over. If it moves I'll naturally adjust to it. If I had a more aggressive mindset then I would be in a better position to put that ball away.' So after every ball I was critiquing myself. 'Was I aggressive when the ball was released? Did I throw that word in?' I wanted to have that aggressive intent so that I could access all of my skills in my unconscious mind.

I was trying to pull myself into the zone and be present for every ball. There was a moment where the little birdie bobbed up on my shoulder. I was going through my checklists correctly, but the scoreboard was going nowhere. At one stage in the fourth over, I was 0 off 10 balls and we were 0 for 16 chasing 179. I was stuck. Off the last ball of the 4th over, my opening partner and great friend, Faf du Plessis, got out. He charged down the track to fast bowler Sandeep Sharma and mishit a slower ball straight up in the air. That little voice on my shoulder grew louder. 'I've caused that,' the voice was saying. 'Me being stuck here is the reason why Faf took a risk he didn't have to take and got out.' It would have been very easy to hear that voice and start digging. But I remembered rule number 1 of the mental road – *If you want to climb out of a hole, the very first thing you must do is stop digging.* I listened to my thoughts and realised what the negativity in that little voice was doing. I realised that it wasn't good and it wasn't going to help me. I knew that I had to keep pulling myself back to the present. This was the only way to dig myself out of the hole and dig my team out of the hole. I was very aware of the shovel being present. So I redirected my thoughts back into what I needed to do right now, and back into my technical and mental process.

Once I got myself back into that zone, things started to really flow. A few B factors lined up for me. A couple of mishits fell into the gap to get me going. Then a couple of good match-ups came my way. Sunrisers bowled Sandeep for back-to-back overs in the powerplay. I scored a boundary off him in the fourth over, when Faf got out. I then hit a four and a six in the sixth over off Sandeep to get my strike-rate back above 100. Sunrisers also used Siddarth Kaul for back-to-back overs outside the powerplay, and he was also a good match-up for me. I got a couple of balls in the slot and was able to put them away. Because I was continually going back through my technical and mental checklists, jamming the song in my head to stay neutral in between balls, and ensuring I remained aggressive at the point of release, I was able to get into the zone and stay there. Those things were my only focus. I was able to tap into my gut feel, trust that the match-ups were right for me, and then fully commit to it with no fear. And once I got into that space, I stayed there. I kept repeating the process every ball. I didn't get ahead of myself or look back at all. I didn't focus on the result or the scoreboard. I had an awareness of it but I was staying totally present working through my checklists. I did this until the game was done.

The result was I made 117 not out off 57 balls and we chased down 179 with 8 wickets in hand and 9 balls to spare to win the IPL final. I struck 11 fours and 8 sixes, after being 0 off 10. I could have easily kept digging like I did in the 2016

IPL final. Like I had so many times during my international career. But I put the shovel down and I stayed fully committed to the process.

I had conserved my mental energy in the lead-up through being disciplined with my pre-game routine. I stayed totally present and locked in with my checklists, because I had practised them and believed in the power of them. I trusted my gut feel, because I had the right mental environment to allow my unconscious mind to take over, which helped me access all of my technical and tactical skills. I didn't violate the rules of the mental road when I could have very easily, at 0 off 10. And I trusted the performance equation. I brought my best A game, had some B factors fall my way, and got the result I dreamed of.

That game stands out for me as the one where I exorcised the demons from 2016 because I put all the mental and technical pieces in place together at the one time, thanks to all the work I had put in over the years.

Unlike the 16-year-old version of me playing for Queensland in the Under 19s, or the 33-year-old version of me in Test cricket, I was not paralysed by fear.

I had moved from a life with no mental framework or process to fall back on when times got tough or when the road became rocky, to being in a place where I felt no matter what was thrown at me, I could combat it. This incredibly powerful and life-changing framework has continued to enrich my life so significantly where I feel I am so much more present with coaching, parenting and anything else I put my mind to. Now it's my turn to share it with you, so you can unlock your mind to bring the very best you have to every performance in your life.

20

Lessons from Cricketing Greats

Prior to the publication of the first edition of this book, I made a podcast called *Lessons Learnt with the Greats*. It was designed to give people insights from some of the greatest cricketers that I have crossed paths with during my career. I wanted to delve into all aspects of their cricketing journey but focus particularly on the lessons they learnt around mental skills during their incredible careers. There are a number of these powerful insights dispersed throughout this book to reinforce various concepts. But in this chapter, I've detailed the mental performance techniques of 10 cricketing greats along with my reflections on why those particular techniques helped make those players so good, and how you can use those techniques to help you in any aspect of your life.

Kevin Pietersen: a lesson on preparation

Every time I played against Kevin Pietersen, he had this bravado and confidence that was obvious for all to see. He was an enforcer with his body language but also with his skill. That was the way he played when he was at his best, and he was incredibly good in all conditions. He always took the game on.

Because of the skill he had, I thought he was just gifted because obviously he had natural power and natural hand–eye coordination. I understood that all the best players had to work incredibly hard, but because of the natural skill that he had, it looked a bit more raw than some others who were a bit more refined technically.

I played with KP right at the start of his career at Hampshire before he made his England Test debut in 2005. I only played with him for a couple of weeks so I didn't understand the lengths that he went to, to be as good as what he was.

But after talking to him on my podcast, I realised he was incredibly particular and detailed with his preparation. He needed to tick off every box. In his mind, that allowed him to step out onto the ground and be ultra confident and have the bravado he was known for. If he didn't tick off every box in his preparation, then he wasn't able to bring the best version of himself to the contest.

For example, if he was preparing to face a particular spinner, he wouldn't just try to get some practice against a similar type of bowler in the nets to replicate the angle and trajectory. He would actually work through all of his shot options against that bowler. He would diligently practice each shot that he wanted to have in his arsenal so that he felt as prepared as possible for every outcome that eventuated.

This type of training can be hard to do. During my career I did try to replicate certain types of bowling in practice to prepare for certain bowlers. If I was going to face a left-arm bowler, I would try to get someone to throw left-arm or throw from a left-arm angle.

Early in my career, a right-arm bowler like Makhaya Ntini was very unique in that he bowled wide of the crease. I would try to practise against that type of angled delivery in the nets so that I could get a sense of how I could line up against him.

But I didn't practice with the specific detail that KP did. Looking back, there certainly would have been value in doing that. I could have been more thoughtful and targeted in making sure I left no stone unturned.

The value of what KP did was that it gave him the confidence of knowing nothing could surprise him. He was reducing the number of external factors that could influence the result. It didn't guarantee him success. But by ticking every box in his preparation, KP gave himself the best chance to reduce the factors outside of his control. He knew when a bowler came on that he had prepared for all of the possible deliveries that would come his way. He felt like he had seen the questions before the exam. That gave him an inner confidence and he was able to exude that during play.

That is something I learnt later in my career. There are always things that are going to arise that are outside of your control. Your opponents will always have something up their sleeve that has the potential to surprise you and put you in a negative mindset if you haven't prepared for it.

But if you have been diligent in your preparation like KP was, even if it is by mentally visualising options as opposed to physically working through every detail, then you can set yourself up for success. It can give you a confidence that you can sidestep any potential problems that may arise, and redirect any negative thoughts that may pop up as a result.

That is one thing that KP did that all players can learn from. He never appeared to have any doubts creep into his mind. He put that down to his meticulous preparation. Success leaves clues, and Kevin Pietersen was certainly one of the best players that I played against.

Allan Border: a lesson on never being satisfied

Allan Border is the godfather of Australian cricket. He was one of my heroes growing up, especially as a Queenslander. He set the standard for the dominant eras of Australian cricket that followed.

My generation owes a lot to AB. He dug Australian cricket out of the doldrums in the mid-1980s and laid the foundations for the great group of players that followed. Those players then set the standards for future Aussie cricketers, which I was very lucky to be a part of.

AB's mental strength was incredible. He was relentless. He never gave anyone a chance to see any sign of weakness in him. He put it all on the line in every performance. He always brought his best effort to everything, and he was never satisfied. When he made runs, he always thought he should have made more. He never rested on his laurels. There are legendary stories of him driving his team even harder at training when they were doing well.

I had the privilege of speaking to AB a lot during my career, but also on my podcast. Allan Border is now a very gentle man in retirement. But the ruthless streak he had as a player and as a captain was a result of his hatred of losing and his fear of failure.

AB's example of using a fear of failure to fuel him is an important one to look at in detail. You don't want fear of failure creeping into your mind while you are in the middle of your performance. AB talked about some of the things he thought about during his best performances. He would often ask himself, 'Am I watching the ball? Not just a general area of where the ball is being released from. Am I zeroing in on the ball?' He wanted to be watching it closely at high intensity. That is similar to many of the great players. He was putting the ball in his mind at the right time and not thinking about anything else. There was no fear of failure entering his mind at that point.

He also spoke about some techniques he used in between balls to switch off and calm his mind. One of those was deep breathing. It was his way of relaxing and putting his mind on neutral by focusing on his breath. Again, there were no fears entering his mind at that point.

Where he used fear of failure was in his preparation. It's really important to understand the distinction between avoiding those thoughts during your actual performance while sometimes using them to your advantage in your preparation.

AB understood this and he often talked about it. He started his career when Australia was underperforming. They could never beat the mighty West Indies teams, who would always thrash them, and they would often lose to England as well. AB hated losing. He was such a competitor that he used the fear of losing, the fear of failing, and turned it into fuel for his preparation. It gave him the ammunition to ensure that he brought the very best version of himself to every game. He knew it was hard enough to beat those teams with his A game. So he made sure he never turned up with anything less than his A game in terms of the things he could control.

That is why he was so relentless and ruthless in his preparation. He was driven to leave no stone unturned, no box unticked. He demanded the same of his players. He ensured that they never turned up underprepared either. Teams are shaped by the standards their leaders set, and AB set the highest standards he could.

He revealed on the podcast that he didn't believe he was the most talented player going around. He had an unconventional batting technique as a result of being an excellent baseballer as a junior. But he knew what his strengths were. He practised them diligently and he was incredibly disciplined in sticking to his game plan and staying with those strengths.

He demanded that his team keep going through the same process, ball after ball, to keep scoring as many runs as they could. He told them to never be satisfied. He told them never to come in until they were told to come in.

That's why AB was such a great leader. He walked the walk and set an example for others to follow. He led with his actions as well as his words. There is not a single player who played under him that wasn't in awe of him as a leader and didn't follow his advice.

AB understood the difference between process and results. He let the past results fuel the process to ensure he gave himself the best chance to have better results in the future. That is exactly what happened to Australian cricket under his watch as captain. Australia went from an awful team to the best in the world because of AB's attitude and leadership. He is a great person to emulate. Let the fear of failure drive your preparation and then focus on the process in the moment. That's why Allan Border is a legend.

Rahul Dravid: a lesson on re-energising

Playing for India and being expected to perform for that team brings a level of mental pressure that very few people from outside of India will ever get to experience. One of the best players to have ever handled that mental pressure is Rahul Dravid.

He was known as 'the wall' because his defence was so hard to get through, but that nickname also applied to his mental state. It was amazing watching him as an opponent. He didn't need any external cues from the opposition to get him into the right mindset. You could just see from the moment he walked out to bat that he had the intensity he needed. But he also balanced that intensity with the correct focus he needed to perform at his best. It looked like he entered a zone and there was no way anyone or anything could penetrate that zone.

What was most impressive with Rahul was his ability to maintain his focus ball after ball, hour after hour, while also being able to switch on and switch off within that headspace to conserve his mental energy.

I didn't learn about his mental techniques until I played with him at Rajasthan Royals in the IPL, and then spoke to him on my podcast. He revealed that he had actually been exposed to basic mental skills like visualisation and meditation from a very young age through a hockey coach he had when he was a junior. He was able to integrate that coaching into his cricket early on.

That also prompted him to explore books on the subject, but he told me that he found some of the information in those books too complicated to understand and apply to his own game.

Once he had got into international cricket, he felt like he needed to find techniques that would keep him fresh mentally. The pressures of playing for India and being in the spotlight, and the overstimulation that came with international cricket, meant that he needed to find ways to re-energise away from the game.

Meditation and yoga were two things that he turned to. They were things that I also learned to use later in my career, but Rahul used them throughout his journey. He would do yoga and meditate before every single game he played.

But one of the more intriguing things that he found worked really well for him was to have deep and meaningful conversations with people about things other than cricket. It is very easy for cricket to consume you, particular for a player like Rahul. It can not only consume you when you're involved in playing or training, but it can actually dominate your mind outside of those times if you socialise with other cricketers or people who want to talk about the game. You can end up talking and thinking about the game even more. It was an issue during my international career where I was thinking about bowlers and match-ups while I was getting my morning coffee.

Rahul found a few key people in his life who he could turn to at different times and he would have profound conversations not about cricket but about life. One of those key people was Paddy Upton, who was a mentor of ours at Rajasthan and had worked with the India team. But he had others in his life who he could talk to, and it was a way for him to put his mind on neutral at critical times when he needed to get away from the game. He would seek out people wiser than him who had experienced challenging situations in other walks of life, as he was eager to learn from them about how they navigated those situations. Rahul was someone who was always learning and wanting to improve in all aspects of life.

The conversations were a way for him to stay present and be in the moment. They required his full attention and he couldn't let his mind wander and turn his attention to cricket. It was a way for him to relax and be present. He made it a priority too. He understood that life can get busy, especially as India's former captain and now head coach, and there were many other demands on his time. Life can get busy for all of us. He was aware that he needed to set some time aside to have important conversations with people to help him re-energise.

It is something I definitely did not do enough as a player. But now as a coach I am very aware of the importance of conversations like these for younger players. Rahul is aware of this too in his coaching career and he is having great success. It's one of the most important things that I do now as a coach. I try to stimulate those types of conversations with players or encourage them to have conversations with people about life in general.

Being present and engaging with people in a meaningful way can be so beneficial for our mental state. It can set you up for success. Rahul Dravid is proof of that.

Lisa Sthalekar: a lesson on observing

Lisa Sthalekar is someone I have admired for many years, and we have got to know each other well while working together on the board of the Australian Cricketers' Association. The former Australia captain and I are a similar age and our international careers ran almost parallel with one another. We also had similar roles as players. She was a spin-bowling all-rounder who had a huge workload in the Australian women's team in all three forms. She consistently batted in the top five, making Test and ODI centuries, while also bowling a lot of overs as the first-choice offspinner. On top of that, she also captained on occasions. They were challenges that I can certainly identify with.

I had the privilege of speaking to Lisa on my podcast about some of the skills she employed to maintain her mental energy during games with such a heavy workload.

I was really interested to learn that her dad was a sports psychologist. From a very young age she got taught some simple techniques around mental rehearsal and visualisation. She also revealed he helped her with some hypnosis techniques to help her get over any mental hurdles. As a kid she was lucky enough to develop the mental skills at the same time as she was learning to play the game.

One thing that really impressed me about Lisa was her understanding of how to switch on and switch off at the right times. It is critical for an allrounder to have that ability because you are involved in the game a lot, and without being able to switch off, you can get mentally fatigued.

This is a consistent theme among successful people in any walk of life, and something that recurs a lot in my coaching and consulting now. The understanding that the brain is a muscle is such an important concept. If you try to keep it activated for long periods, you will wear it out.

Lisa used to use a similar technique that I did in terms of playing a song in her head in between deliveries. She said she knew she was having a good day if she was able to play a song in her head consistently. But she also revealed that she wasn't able to do that all the time.

When she struggled to play a song in her head, she found another method to switch off and ensure she wasn't overthinking things and burning mental energy. She would actually take her mind outside the ground and focus on her family in the crowd. In between balls she would observe their movements. Just by observing what they were doing and remaining present, it gave her some relief from the intense focus she needed when she was bowling, batting or fielding. This is a really interesting and very simple method to put your mind on neutral.

She revealed that there were times, speaking to her mum, dad or sister after a game, when she would ask them about specific incidents that happened to them during the day, and they were surprised about how much detail she had and how closely she was watching them. But it was an anchor for her.

Some might wonder whether a technique like this would actually burn more mental energy. But she wasn't using an intense focus when observing her family. It was a general awareness. What she was doing was putting her mind on something else for a few moments in between balls. By thinking about something else, there was no possible way for any negative cricket thoughts to pop into her head. She couldn't get anxious or overthink a situation when she was bowling, batting or captaining her team. It was a way of putting her mind on neutral in the same way that singing a song in her head would do.

I had another player I coached in the IPL reveal that there have been days when he was at his best when he would look into the stands and place his awareness on some fans or something random that was happening up there. There have been other players who would stare into the distance to find an object as far away as they could see.

Lisa's example is a really good one in that she was able to find another method if her first one wasn't working. Having multiple anchors to turn to can be beneficial to help find a neutral place and conserve your mental energy if you are having trouble on a certain day.

Given Lisa's grounding with her mental skills from a young age and her understanding of how to switch on and off during her career, it is no surprise that she was such a consistent all-round performer for Australia over a decade-long international career. It gave Lisa Sthalekar the best chance to let her skillset shine across her batting, bowling and in the field.

Sir Vivian Richards: a lesson on being fully present

Sir Isaac Vivian Richards had it all. He was one of the biggest enforcers to ever play the game of cricket. He was a street fighter and he had that trademark swagger, that presence at the crease. He always got into the contest and didn't want to be beaten. He was ruthless.

I remember watching Viv as a kid. The West Indies cap, the gold chain, the chewing gum. He was the king of cool.

But it wasn't until I had the great privilege to speak to him on my podcast that I realised that the chewing gum wasn't just part of the look.

Viv famously never wore a helmet. He did reveal he wore a mouth guard for a brief period early in his career but had done away with it. He replaced it with chewing gum. But it wasn't to look cool. It helped his mental performance. He spoke about how the rhythm of chewing gum anchored him in that flow state. It kept him calm. He would chew gum in rhythm with tapping his bat. It kept him present and focused and ready to dominate some of the best fast bowlers of all time.

For him to understand he needed that rhythm, a place to anchor his thoughts, to keep him present, is undoubtedly one of the things that made him one of the all-time greats. Every human being and every cricketer needs to understand exactly what their anchor is to be able to get them into that headspace where they're at ease, where they're at peace, where they can put their mind on neutral and just come back to being fully present.

Viv only realised that after not chewing gum early in his career. He realised it was actually critical to his performance. It's so simple. It's hard to believe a piece of chewing gum could have such an impact. But if you watch highlights of Viv playing, you can see the impact it had on his rhythm, his calmness, his ability to stay present as the bowler was running in.

Viv wasn't the only cricketer I came across who chewed gum to help anchor them in the present. I remember speaking to former Australia T20 player Ben Dunk about this. I played a game against him in the Pakistan Super League in 2020. He was playing for Lahore Qalandars against my team, Quetta Gladiators. He made 93 not out from 43 balls with 10 sixes. It's as good an innings as I've seen against some quality bowlers. I'd never seen him play like that before. He was like Matt

Hayden in the way he batted. I remember he was chewing gum and he kept blowing bubbles after every ball. I'd never seen that from him before either. I asked him after the game what was happening with the chewing gum, knowing at this stage of my career that people like Viv, and others, had used it as a mental anchor. He confirmed that he'd been working with a mental coach and that it was a way for him to stay present, by just thinking about blowing bubbles.

Chewing gum wasn't the anchor I used later in my career. Some people use breathing techniques. I used music as a way to anchor my thoughts. I love music, and once I understood the need to use a technique to put my mind on neutral, I thought back to some of my best performances earlier in my career and remembered that I was playing a song in my head during those performances. It was a technique that two of my teammates, Glenn McGrath and Michael Clarke, had used and both were incredibly successful.

I still use that technique now in other parts of my life if I need to put my mind on neutral. It ensures I don't burn through mental energy unnecessarily by letting other thoughts enter my mind.

People just need to try what's most comfortable, most natural for them to be able to pull themselves back to the present.

Chewing gum is a really simple technique. If it's good enough for Sir Viv Richards, it might be good enough for you.

So once you know exactly what that anchor is for you, then that's when you give yourself the best chance to be able to make the most of your good days, and Sir Viv Richards certainly knew how to make the most of his good days.

Matthew Hayden: a lesson in 'do mode' visualisation

Matthew Hayden was one of the most imposing players I ever played with. But it wasn't just his physical presence and raw skill that made him great. What people probably don't know about Haydos is how well-honed his mental skills were, particularly around using visualisation and imagery when preparing for games, from a first-person or 'do mode' perspective.

You may have seen photos or vision of Haydos the day before a Test match, sitting on the pitch with his shoes off, gloves and bat in hand and his eyes closed.

I remember it so clearly before every Test match that I was involved in with Haydos, either as a teammate or squad member. He often wouldn't hit balls in the nets during the optional training session the day before a game. Instead, he would spend around 45 minutes just sitting on the pitch.

What he was doing was tapping into the power of imagery. He later explained to me that he was working through a visualisation of what was going to unfold the following day. He wanted to take in all the surroundings and really get into that headspace.

When I learnt more about this technique from Jacques, which he called 'do mode' – visualising doing something through your own eyes – I understood the power of it.

Haydos was seeing each bowler he was going to come up against and imagining the ball coming down at him. He was imagining how the bowlers were trying to get him out and how he would react if they bowled balls in certain areas.

Compared to other players that I played with, Haydos was certainly someone who tapped into the power of imagery more than most, and that was his perfect preparation.

For Haydos, using imagery like this meant that when he went into the game, and was actually in the moment of competition itself, it felt like it was not the first time he had seen the ball come down at him standing in that spot, in that stadium, against that bowler. He had already gone through that situation in his mind and imagined how he was going to handle it.

From what I now know about this technique, that type of practice lays down the foundations of muscle memory that we have as human beings. It really starts to build those neural pathways and refreshes your mind on how you are going to react. It pre-programmes your body to be on autopilot, because you have seen it before.

When I played with Haydos early in my international career, I didn't understand the power of tapping into that. I certainly wish I did. I was a player who would go to the nets and hit balls to try to replicate what might be coming up in the game. There was nothing wrong with that. But I didn't understand how incredibly powerful it is for you to be able to actually get into your mind, get into 'do mode' through your own eyes and start that preparation phase, to make sure that your muscle memory and your neural pathways are primed for you to be able to react instinctively.

As powerful a mental technique as it is, Haydos also understood the importance of doing this practice at the right time. It's not something you want to do too much of on the morning of a game because that can deplete your mental energy. But implementing it at the right time like he did, the day before a game, you could see why he was so dominant, because he was not just using all aspects of his cricket skill but also tapping into the power of his mind.

The power of imagery set him up for success when he was in the middle during a Test match. His body was not feeling like it was doing something for the first time, which allowed him to stay totally present out there. He also explained to me that he never used to look at the scoreboard. Those two strategies meant that he never allowed any outside thoughts to infiltrate his mind during a match.

He had immense technical skill, which had come from years of hard work, but when it was packaged with the mental skills he had developed over his career, you could see why Matthew Hayden became one of Australia's all-time greats.

Brett Lee: a less on 'view mode' visualisation

Brett Lee was one of my favourite teammates, but he used to do something before games that I thought was incredibly self-indulgent. Yet, in hindsight, it was pure genius.

I remember the first time I saw it like it was yesterday. It was the 2006 Champions Trophy in India, and we were in Mohali. We were about to play India. They had Virender Sehwag, who, for any opening bowler in that era, was one of the most fearsome opponents you could come up against. He was unbelievably good. He would take the bowlers on from ball one.

I remember sitting in the team bus on the way to the ground. Our team analyst had given Binga a device to watch some vision. Everyone expected him to be looking at footage of Sehwag, seeing how he had got out so he could formulate what his plans would be. But no, Binga wasn't watching Sehwag. I was sitting near him on the bus and I could see him watching highlights of himself clean bowling batters, ripping stumps out of the ground, celebrating with his trademark chainsaw and jumping up and down.

I remember saying, 'Binga, what the hell are you doing?' Everyone on the bus was laughing and taking the piss out of him watching his own highlights. Everyone thought he was just doing it to pump himself up, having not done the right preparation in terms of watching vision of his opponents. Everyone thought that Binga only had plan A, which was bowling 150 kph outswingers, or plan B, which was yorkers and bouncers.

I didn't ask Binga at the time *why* he did it. I didn't ask the great players that I played with exactly why they did things and what their thoughts were. I was so naive.

But Binga later revealed to me that he was only doing it to be able to step into the very best version of himself, to see the intensity that he had, to see what he was doing when he was at his absolute best.

Most people tend to pigeonhole fast bowlers and believe that they don't really think that much and that they're not the smartest players on the team. But Brett Lee really understood how to get himself into the right mindset.

He talked about it on my podcast, saying that he used to trick himself into thinking that he had just come off a five-wicket haul. Even if he had come off a poor game or a long injury layoff, he could put his mind in a place where he believed he was at his best by watching vision of himself being successful. It reconfirmed what his best looked like and put him in the right headspace to find that intensity straight away.

It's no secret now as to why Brett Lee was as good as he was for so long. He was athletically gifted and worked extremely hard, but he also knew how to harness the mental side of the game by watching footage of himself at his absolute best so that he was ready to step out in a big game, in a World Cup or Champions Trophy, and immediately tap into the best version of himself.

One of the weapons that he had from ball one was that he was on the money. I remember him getting Chris Gayle out a few times first ball because he was ready to go and he knew the intensity level that he needed.

I wish I'd known why he watched vision of himself, when I played with him, because I certainly did not watch footage of myself at my best when I was younger, unless I was desperate and had been struggling for quite a while. That would be the only time I thought I needed to see what the best version of me looked like.

Once I knew the power of this after talking to Jacques, the power of what he described as 'view mode' visualisation, I would do this as part of my pre-game routine. Through watching vision of me at my best, I could see what my technical movement patterns were but also what my intensity levels were like. I always had an aggressive intent at my best, and by seeing that in highlights it would prompt me to recreate it when I went out to play.

Now as a coach, one of the first things I ask players is whether they watch vision of themselves at their best. Most say they don't. Most are like I was when I was younger, and only watch vision when they are struggling, instead of doing it regularly to limit the chances of falling into a rut and to get constant reminders of what they do at their best from a technical and mental perspective.

Binga was a genius. People thought he didn't think a lot about the game. They thought that he was just athletically and technically gifted and that he loved the big occasion. But there were so many more layers to him on the mental side of the game. Brett Lee had just about everyone fooled.

Ricky Ponting: a lesson on thought sequence

I played so much cricket with Ricky Ponting and was very grateful that he was both my captain and a playing mentor for a large portion of my international career. But it was only after my playing career had finished that I learnt the details of his thought process when facing up to a bowler in a game.

It's probably one of the biggest disappointments for me looking back on my playing career that I didn't ask him about it at the time. But when I interviewed him on my podcast, *Lessons Learnt with the Greats*, he opened up about the exact thoughts he put in his mind as the bowler was running in.

Ricky explained that he had a very deliberate routine every ball. He would say 'watch the ball' to himself three times. First, as the bowler started his run up; second, as the bowler was halfway in; and third, as the bowler was in his delivery stride. He knew that by putting that thought into his mind that the wrong thought couldn't intrude. I'm not sure if Ricky fully understood rule number two of the ACT Model, that your mind can only actively process one thought at a time. But he intuitively realised that if he put that sequence of thoughts in his mind as the bowler was running in, then any negative thoughts couldn't distract him.

The thoughts he didn't want to infiltrate his mind were around the situation of the game, or premeditated thoughts like, 'Can I get a shorter length to be able to pull on the back foot?'

When he explained his thought process, it was a huge lightbulb moment for me. It confirmed what I had been taught by Jacques about putting the right thoughts in your head at the right time.

Ricky's sequence of thoughts was just as important as the thought itself. It's not just about putting the right thought in as the ball comes down, or as you release the ball if you are a bowler. It's also about what your individual sequence of thoughts is as the bowler starts to run in, or as you start to run in as a bowler, and what is happening in your mind in between balls.

Ricky repeated the same thought, 'watch the ball', to keep it clear and simple. But for me, I did it slightly differently while using the same principles of putting the right thought in at the right time.

As the bowler was starting to run in, I worked through my technical checklist and continued that as the bowler was getting into his load-up. Then, as the ball was released, I put the word 'aggressive' into my mind at the right time.

Even before I asked Ricky about his process, that was the sequence I'd put into place at the back end of my career because of what I was taught by Jacques.

He was also fanatical about keeping the pitch clean around the crease line where he would take his stance. For him, that was his 'office' and he wanted to keep it tidy. Again, without necessarily knowing why, it was a way of putting his mind on neutral to ensure negative thoughts didn't pop in between balls.

In hindsight, it is enlightening to look back at these things because I developed similar habits in my routines in between balls after bedding down my ACT Model. I would quickly analyse how I handled the delivery based on my process but then I would put my mind on neutral by playing a song in my head while the bowler walked back to his mark. The song was my version of Ricky's gardening. It put my mind on neutral and conserved my mental energy.

Ricky was able to keep the right sequence of thoughts going through his mind for long periods in Test matches. That was one of his superpowers. He was unrelenting. He was able to maintain that intensity, ball after ball, for hours and days. But this is because he had a way to be able to shut it down in between balls and maintain his mental energy so he could continue to react to the best of his ability each ball. There was not one ball where he wasn't fully engaged in the competition. Developing the right sequence of thoughts and putting them in your mind at the right time is a vital lesson to learn from a player as great as Ricky Ponting.

AB de Villiers: a lesson on intensity and performance

AB de Villiers is a superhero. Some of his batting looked superhuman at times. He left you in awe of his ability. It seemed at times like the bowlers were bowling in slow motion to him.

Some of the fastest and best bowlers were made to look slow and pedestrian by AB.

I played a lot against him during my career and he struck a lot of fear into me as an opponent. But I got to know him a lot more when I played with him at Royal Challengers Bangalore in the IPL. He is a very sweet and gentle man.

It was interesting to learn from him on my podcast how he turned himself into that superhero. He spoke about having to find the right intensity for him to be at his absolute best. For him it was very high and that is hard to sustain.

One of the methods he would use to try to put himself in that state was to imagine he was acting out a movie and playing the lead role. For him to be at his absolute best, he needed to feel like he was acting in order to put his mind in a place where he could convince himself he was invincible.

There were times where he found that level playing against Australia. He mentioned he found that level in his last ever Test series in 2018. He was facing Pat Cummins, Mitchell Starc, Josh Hazlewood and Nathan Lyon, and he made sure he was the lead role in his movie. He felt like the ball and the whole game slowed down for him. Watching him bat when he was in that invincible mode was something else.

There was another series in 2014 when I was in the Australian squad where he found this level. It was a game at Centurion when Mitchell Johnson was bowling at his absolute quickest. I wasn't playing in the game, but I was watching intently. Mitch took 12 wickets in the match and was terrorising all of South Africa's batters except for AB. He found that intensity level that he needed to match Mitch and was going toe-to-toe with him – just like a superhero and a villain in a movie. I remember AB playing this back-foot drive off one of Mitch's rockets, which AB made look like a slower ball.

While AB tried to play the lead role in his own movie, he didn't necessarily show it externally. As an opponent, it looked like he created a bubble around himself. He didn't make eye contact with the bowler. He always turned his back after the ball was bowled. He didn't need external stimulation to hit that right intensity level. But he obviously found a way to get himself there in his own mind.

That is a good lesson for all of us. A lot of players I coach now want to find that level of confidence or invincibility. It can be hard to find; you need to find the right internal cue for you and it may not look the same for everyone depending on the level of intensity you need.

AB revealed that it was hard for him to find that level of intensity all the time and there were other days where he needed to bring his best without being able to play the lead role in his own movie.

He recalled his famous 2015 World Cup innings against West Indies in Sydney as one of those times. AB made one of the fastest ever World Cup centuries off just 52 balls. He ended up making 162 not out off 66 balls. But he revealed he was not feeling well before he went out to bat. He said the night before he had been really sick and did not sleep much. Before he went out to bat, he was lying on a massage table feeling crook.

He was not able to get his mind to a place where he could play that lead role. Instead, he had to take the attitude that he had nothing to lose. He played almost care free because he was distracted by his illness and, surprisingly, delivered one of his greatest performances.

I remember having a similar experience in making my highest ever ODI score against Bangladesh in Dhaka. We had fielded first in incredibly hot conditions. I had bowled seven overs and felt cooked when I went out to open the batting. I decided I wasn't going to run much. I thought I would just load up, fully let go with no fear and see how I went. I got 185 not out off 96 balls. I remember thinking, 'Where the hell did that come from and why can't I do that more often?'

It was such a valuable point that AB raised about his innings against West Indies. There is a really thin line between fully letting go and not caring at all. He was able to identify where that right intensity was for him in that moment without being reckless.

That's what made AB such a special player. He could produce superhuman performances in different ways and it is a good lesson to learn that you won't always have the perfect mindset. While he wanted to play the lead role in a movie and find that ultra-high intensity that put him in a position to play some of the most amazing Test innings we have ever seen, he couldn't always recreate that in his own mind. There were days when he wasn't feeling good and he still had to deliver for his team. AB de Villiers was able to let go of that high intensity and play with freedom. His adaptability was his superpower.

Justin Langer: a lesson on letting go

Justin Langer was one of the most intensely focused people I ever played with. He was a shining example of how to bring the best version of yourself to every game. Never once was he not fully focused, not fully locked into the contest.

But one thing JL revealed to me after his career was finished was how he learned to balance out his intensity by letting go. He spoke on my podcast about how important it was for him to learn how to let go of his intense and often self-destructive desire to control the outcome, and just enjoy the game and take it on without fearing failure.

On one of his early tours with the Australian Test team in 1993, he told me that he had had a conversation with New Zealand batter John Wright. John was a very successful Test batter and would later go on to have a great career as an international coach.

Wright said to JL during this tour, 'You just look like you're wanting it too much. You look like you've got the weight of the world on your shoulders. You have to let go.'

JL said it took him quite a few years to really understand this advice. The lightbulb moment came for him during the 2001 Ashes series when he felt like he had hit rock bottom. He couldn't score any runs and had been dropped from the Test team. He was unsure if he would get another chance to play for Australia. But out of nowhere an opportunity to play late in that series presented itself, and he knew that was the time he needed to just let go of his fixation on results and play with freedom.

I remember watching him in 2001 and then beyond when I started to tour with the Australian team in 2002, and you could see the shift he'd made. He went from being a grinder, intent on not getting out, to letting go and dominating some of the partnerships he had with Matthew Hayden. You could see the joy on his face and it coincided with the best performances of his career. His transformation is a real lesson for all of us.

Like JL, I always believed that hard work, sheer intensity and desperation for results should be rewarded. But when you don't get those results, that desperation keeps compounding pressure on yourself. Once I understood that I could only prepare as best as I could and then enjoy the moment of competition while letting go of the possible outcome, what I could achieve became pretty amazing.

One of the methods JL used to start letting go and easing the burden in his mind was transcendental meditation. John Wright had suggested this to him as a way to unload the thoughts that were consuming him. It was a way to redirect his mind back to the present and regenerate his mental energy. JL revealed to me that it is something he still does every day for just 15 or 20 minutes, and it makes him feel better whenever he's stressed or anxious.

Transcendental meditation is something I learnt to use later in my career after being directed to it by one of my mentors, Paddy Upton. Like JL, I found it a very powerful tool.

JL also revealed that it wasn't just John Wright that had first clued him in to the concept of letting go. He remembered conversations he used to have with his nanna when he was worried about something as a young boy. She would ask him a simple question each time: 'Can you control that?' He would always respond with, 'Well, no I can't.' Quick as a flash she would say to him, 'Well then, don't worry about it. If you can control it, then do something about it. But if you can't control it, don't worry about it.'

It took JL a while to really embrace that concept from his nanna, but they were wise words. They reminded me of one of the most important questions that I have ever been asked, which was, 'When has worrying about the result ever made the result better?'

The answer to that question is never. Why do we spend so much time worrying about things that are out of our control? It was something that consumed me for large parts of my career and in other aspects of my life as well. Once I learned to let go of that worry and let go of my fixation on results, then it felt like the weight of the world had been lifted off my shoulders.

It was a valuable lesson that I learnt, and it mirrored the lessons JL learned from John Wright and his nanna. JL may not have made the transformation he did without listening to their advice. Thankfully for Australian cricket he did, because it helped Justin Langer become one of our best Test openers and an inspirational teammate to play alongside.

* * *

Hopefully, you can apply some of the lessons from these great cricketers to help you create a winner's mindset. You now have the tools to bring the best version of you to every performance.

Acknowledgements

Putting this book together wouldn't have been possible without the help and guidance of a number of very special people. First of all, I need to thank my incredible wife Lee for her unconditional love and support and for giving me the encouragement to get my thoughts in order.

Will Power, the great Australian export, you were a godsend!! None of this would have been possible without your counsel, guidance and connection with Dr Jacques Dallaire.

I am immensely grateful to Dr Jacques Dallaire, who has been so generous and kind in sharing all the knowledge and wisdom that he has gained over his years of working with people who are pushing the human limits to be the best they can be.

Helping me every step of the way in crafting this book has been the patient and gifted Alex Malcolm. I can't thank Alex enough for his time and dedication to bring my ideas to life.

I have been very fortunate in my life to be mentored by some of the true masters of their craft, and Gideon Haigh is certainly one of these. I have always admired Gideon's incredible use of the English language in his writing, so his finishing touches on ensuring that this book reads as I dreamed it to, is so appreciated.

I need to thank Helen Littleton at HarperCollins Australia and Sachin Sharma at HarperCollins India for believing in my vision to ensure everyone around the world has access to one of the most essential life skills that we all are trying to master.

And finally, my greatest thanks of all, is to all of the wonderful people who supported me throughout my playing days: my coaches, teammates and, above all, the cricket-loving public. This book is the outcome of the incredible journey that I have been on and what it has taught me. I hope you benefit from some of the lessons I have learned in navigating this very exciting but always challenging life that we live.

About the author

Shane Watson is one of the world's leading cricket coaches and mentors, and spends his year travelling the world working with some of the best cricketers and athletes in the world. Shane's unique style of coaching separates him from his peers as his coaching philosophy focuses on this invaluable mental skills framework which has seen many cricketers and sporting teams go on to achieve their full potential and have tremendous success.